VOL. 3

Soul Talk

VOL. 3

Soul Talk

SOUL-STIRRING STORIES OF PEOPLE
WHO LET GO AND LET GOD

CHERYL POLOTE-WILLIAMSON

purposely
created
PUBLISHING

SOUL TALK, VOL. 3
Published by Purposely Created Publishing Group™
Copyright © 2019 Cheryl Polote-Williamson
All rights reserved.

Printed in the United States of America

ISBN: 978-1-64484-125-9

Special discounts are available on bulk quantity purchases by book clubs, associations and special interest groups. For details email: sales@publishyourgift.com or call (888) 949-6228.

For information logon to: www.PublishYourGift.com

Dedication

This book is dedicated to the many people who struggle with letting go and letting God.

In Him,
Cheryl Polote-Williamson

Table of Contents

Foreword

As I sit this evening in a stormy airport listening to the wind and the rain, I can't help but think about the stories that you're about to experience in *Soul Talk, Volume III.* The storms of life have tried to destroy so many of our storytellers. The winds have blown a few off course. The uncontrollable rain of tears has soaked them. Yet, through it all, God has shown Himself faithful. He is still saying, "Peace. Be still." As you are about to discover, God is still delivering His people.

I am honored to recommend this life-changing anthology. My friend Cheryl Polote-Williamson is allowing the Lord to use her in a unique way to transform lives.

I knew there was something very special about Cheryl when we met in June 2018. Our spirits connected. While greeting many people at a women's leadership conference, the Lord brought Cheryl clearly into view. I caught her attention and stepped out of the receiving line to meet her. And more important than just meeting her, I conveyed to her that God had a greater work for her to do. I had no knowledge of her work, let alone a "greater" work. I didn't know Cheryl. But I did know the voice of the Lord, and I was obedient to what He told me to do and say.

So, the Lord put us together for His good. While others were lined up to meet me, the Lord wanted me to meet Cheryl. We became instant best friends. She has poured into my life. Cheryl loves God and she loves His people.

My prayer for Cheryl is that she remains obedient to the call of God and continues to tell our stories. My prayer for you is that you will be changed by these stories, touched by these people's journeys, and lift your hands or bend your knees in awe of God's relentless pursuit of His children.

Settle in. Listen up.

It's time for some *Soul Talk, Volume III.*

Cynt Marshall
CEO, Dallas Mavericks
Founder, President, and CEO, Marshalling Resources
Retired AT&T Executive

Pain Is Profitable

NWANYE DAVIS-BARNES

*"So do not throw away your confidence; it
will be richly rewarded."*

—Hebrews 10:35 (NIV)

Pain is profitable. I'm not talking about the pain we allow for convenience; I'm talking about the kind of pain that shows up without your permission. It didn't ask if it was ok to interrupt your life, it just showed up. You wake up one day and it's sitting on the side of your bed or you come home from a beautiful vacation and it's in your living room as you walk in the door or like in my case you're born and one of your first memories as a child is being introduced to pain. No warning, no one asked your permission; pain has showed up and life as you know it has changed—in that very moment—forever.

When I think back over my life, it was two-dimensional; I literally lived in two worlds.

Many of us can remember at what age our first memory was formed. I was four years old when I heard a knock on the door, I heard my mother answer, and when I peeked out of my bedroom to see who it was I saw a tall, handsome man who looked like a giant; this tall, gentle giant would later become my stepfather. (Dimension one.)

The second memory I have is at age five on Christmas Eve. We're all at my aunt's house. I'm there with my mother, sister, cousins, aunts, uncles, everyone you would expect at your family gathering on Christmas Eve. We're all celebrating, laughing, singing, and dancing. Then, BOOM... Pain shows up!

Sometimes (although I can't remember) I wonder if I was afraid. Maybe I wasn't because Pain was tall in stature and the same complexion as my dad—who was one of the most loving men I would ever come to know. It's very possible that I recognized Pain and was terrified that no one intervened when he said I had to go with him that night. Either way, Pain showed up in my life at five years old and I would never be the same again.

My aunt's husband (who we will call Pain) was going to the store and he invited me to go with him. No one asked why, not even me; everyone kept on partying and enjoying the celebration as Pain took me by the hand and led me to his car. I had on a beautiful Christmas Eve dress with pretty lace white socks; that is a detail I will never forget. Pain drove a white sports car that night and off to the store we went. During that ride, Pain pulled over on the side of a dark street and forced me to do things that no child should ever have to endure. I was raped that night and it wouldn't be the last time. (Dimension two.)

For eight years, I would go on to live in two dimensions. Two different worlds, so to speak. One world was normal, beautiful, and peaceful with my stepdad; the other was evil, cruel, scary, and perverted with my aunt's husband who (I assume) was given permission to do whatever he wanted whenever he wanted.

I don't know this for certain, but I believe I was being sold to that demon.

Only by God's grace am I able to share my story in hopes that it not only brings awareness to parents that pedophiles don't always look like what you see in a movie but to also show survivors of abuse of any kind that God can heal and deliver you from pain.

I sit here at this moment, 3:33 a.m., to let you know God is a healer, deliverer, redeemer, and among many other things a restorer. It is no surprise that after suffering something this traumatic, my reason for living became very confusing. On Saturdays, I would go to TG&Y with my stepdad and buy a new Barbie doll, but by the next week my mother was dropping me off with Pain where I would endure the unthinkable.

For years, I found myself going to school during the week and spending memorable Saturdays with my stepdad all the while cringing at the very thought of ever seeing Pain again, hoping the last time was *the last time*.

I lived in this weird space never really knowing why or how this could happen to me. As you can, imagine I had a lot of questions that no one has ever answered, probably because I never required them to.

Needless to say, my life as a child was seemingly lived as an adult. I became the protector of all those who didn't protect me. I sometimes wonder how I look on that life-altering, horrific Christmas Eve night back in 1978. Were my clothes wrinkled? Were they stained? Did I smell funny? In that defining moment, I became a protector; I didn't want to ruin anyone's Christmas Eve.

Everyone was so happy. I certainly couldn't tell anyone. Who would believe me? What would happen to our family? My dad would kill him and spend the rest of his life in prison and my *normal, beautiful, peaceful* world would end. My mother would be guilt-ridden forever for letting me go with that deranged man, and my aunt would be divorced and her rich, lavish lifestyle would end (so I thought).

So, I kept that horrible secret and many more only to protect the very lives responsible for ruining mine. As I grew up, I began to ask myself questions I should have been asking my mother, like, why was I with that man? How did I get there? Who picked me up?

Why? Why? Why?

I'm 46 years old and I still haven't asked her those questions. I've tried, I have hinted, but remember I'm a protector now and what's the point in ruining her life with questions I already know the answers to?

1994 was the first time I would ever admit to anyone I was molested, raped, and stripped of who I was meant to be. We were at a gas station on our way home from my grand-parents' house. While I was pumping gas, I casually said, "Mom, I was molested by Pain." Her response kept me quiet for 20 more years. I was 21 years old then, and I was broken, confused, denied, and rejected.

We drove home never to speak of it again, not the way I needed to speak about it. At that very moment, I allowed **pain** to become a part of my life like it was my skin color. I didn't have the tools to get this dysfunction out of my life, never fully understanding that the freedom I so desired was inside of me; after all, I had provided freedom to so many others. I carried this burden so that they could be free, why couldn't I free myself? Why wouldn't I offer myself the same freedom I offered to everyone else?

So, I spent 40 years begging for something that was already on the inside of me. It's very similar to the people of Israel. Pain showed up uninvited and they married it for 40 years, never fully understanding that God had already put freedom on the inside of them. What should've taken 11 days took 40 years. I can certainly say the same for me. Please understand that I am in no way excusing those responsible for abusing me or those who allowed the abuse, and I'm certainly not insinuating a victim of abuse (at any age) should be able to find their freedom quickly.

I am simply saying that on the day I was introduced to Jesus Christ by my grandmother, He began to love me and introduced me to the freedom that was inside of me. Of course, by then Pain had painted trauma on me like it was my skin color; it belonged to me. I took it with me everywhere I went. I took it to high school, my jobs, college, relationships—I raised my children with it. I even had it with me on my wedding day. My name may as well have been Jabez (1 Chronicles 4:9-10), for obvious reasons.

Little did I know my story was just getting started. During my next 20 years of silence, I began to listen to the lies of the enemy that told me I wasn't good enough and I believed *this was all there was*. The abuse, betrayal, and lies would be my life. And when (or if) I get to Heaven, I can rest then.

I began to question everything and everyone in my life including God. Someone owed me answers and I got them, just not in the way I thought I would nor were they the answers to the obvious questions I had. Instead of God telling me why that horrible night had to happen and why I had to endure years of a sexual predator, He began telling me who I really was, why I was here, and why He required me to write my story in this particular book.

As you begin to understand and accept God's plan for your life, you will focus more on the Who (Jesus) and not the why. Many times, we tend to focus on the destination not the journey.

Had I spent my time focusing on who God was in my life and who I am in Him, I could have gotten to my freedom, my healing, and my deliverance a lot sooner.

Trauma of any kind is difficult to understand. Many of us have experienced unbearable and unspeakable pain, but rest assured that at this level, pain is profitable in the lives of Christians. The level of trauma I endured, and need I say survived, has and will continue to benefit so many others. You will profit from my story and others will profit from yours. God will never leave us nor forsake us (Hebrews 13:5). I am a living witness that trauma (although strong enough to do so) does not have to end your life; it is just as powerful to propel you into your destiny.

Jabez defied his hopeless name and dysfunctional beginning to become someone who believed fervently in the power of God. Jabez was honored because of his relationship with God (1 Chronicles 4:9), not because of who his parents were, where he was born, or what his name was.

This is not the end of my story. Forgiving Pain and those responsible for the trauma in my life is just the beginning. I learned how to forgive yesterday, I am learning how to do it again today, and I will practice doing it tomorrow. For you, forgiveness may be like it is for me... daily.

The two important lessons I learned about forgiveness are: forgiveness doesn't have to wait on an apology nor does forgiving someone mean I have to grant them access into my life again.

All that I have endured led me to the Lord, who I must introduce you to—"If you declare with your mouth, 'Jesus is Lord,' and believe in your heart that God raised him from the dead, you will be saved. For it is with your heart that you believe and are justified, and it is with your mouth that you profess your faith and are saved." (Romans 10:9-10, NIV)

If you would like to accept Jesus Christ into your life as your personal Lord and Savior to help guide you through your journey regardless of what season you are in right now, please pray this prayer with me:

Dear Lord Jesus, thank you for dying on the cross for my sins. Please forgive me. I ask that you come into my life. I receive you as my personal Lord and Savior. Now help me to live for You the rest of my life. In Jesus' name I pray. Amen!

May God bless you and keep you in perfect peace all the days of your life.

SOUL REFLECTION:

As a survivor, understand that you already won! You beat the odds—you are still here! By His stripes you are healed! You are an overcomer by the blood of the Lamb and the word of your testimony! Rebuke the lies that come to steal, kill, and destroy what God has put inside of you. You are worthy! You are strong! You are more than enough! You are joint heirs with Christ!

A Peace That Surpasses All Understanding

TYREESE R. MCALLISTER

"And the peace of God, which surpasses all understanding, will guard your hearts and your minds in Christ Jesus."

—Philippians 4:7 (ESV)

A peace that surpasses all understanding is a powerful account of finding peace in the midst of a storm or tragedy. Philippians 4:7 has been a healing balm in Gilead throughout my personal life and during my 25-year crisis counseling career. Many marvel at my ability to remain sane, and first responders appreciate my ability to remain calm and get the job done under pressure. My reputation often preceded my showing up. It often brought a sigh of relief knowing that I can handle the disorganized client, the grieving parent, the profoundly psychotic, or just the nosey spectators. I submit to you that only the peace of God that surpasses all understanding makes this possible.

On March 21, 2017, my life was forever changed by a phone call and Philippians 4:7 was put to the test. My two daughters and their roommate, all college freshmen, were home on spring break. On the evening of March 21, the girls went out with their friends from school.

Due to our busy schedules, my husband, Anthony, and I are rarely home together in the evenings. We had finished dinner and I was preparing lunch for the next day when the phone rang. It was our oldest daughter, Daja. I jokingly said to my husband, "It's your girl wanting to extend the curfew." When I picked up the phone, it disconnected. My husband said, "Call her back, something might be wrong." I replied, "Stop worrying, she may have pocket dialed me." Before I could call her, she called back. When I picked up this time, I heard Daja say, "Mommy, Lolli (Ayana) got shot!" I couldn't believe my ears. Was I dreaming? A stranger took the phone from Daja and confirmed what had happened and that the ambulance was on the scene. We quickly dressed and rushed to the hospital.

"O God, my baby has been shot!" That thought began to flood my mind and trouble my heart. Despite having a master's degree in counseling psychology, completed course work for my doctorate in psychology, and over 25 years of crisis work experience, I was not prepared for this. Trainings on mental wellness, resiliency, trauma treatment, and post-traumatic stress disorder suddenly went on sabbatical. In that moment, I became a breathing, walking, and living testimony of needing the promise of Philippians 4:7— the peace of God to guard my heart and mind in Jesus Christ.

Ayana underwent a twelve-hour surgery. Supporters joined us at the hospital and in prayer. When the surgery was over, the doctor's diagnosis was damage to the heart which resulted in three cardiac arrests. The prognosis the doctor offered was grave and he explained that the next 24 hours were critical. Immediate family was allowed to see her. As I sat by her bed, admiring her beautiful, flawless skin, she appeared to be sleeping peacefully. I held her hand, laughing to myself about how she had gotten her nails manicured just before coming home on spring break. While her body was going through hell, she lay there looking like an angel. This was the real Ayana—full of love, and beautiful inward and outward.

I asked Ayana if she could hear me and she moaned in response. I squeezed her hand three times, which was our code for "I love you." We had this secret code since she was four. She was supposed to squeeze my hand four times indicating, "I love you more." She didn't; instead, she gave me a faint head nod, which I took as "love you more." I replied, "I know." I queued my iPhone playlist up to play her favorite gospel songs and whispered, "Love, fight the good fight." I said to her, "I love you. I can't do this without you. This is not our agreement." While allowing me to bond with my baby in those precious moments, unbeknownst to me, God was preparing Ayana, a lover of the Lord, and me for her flight to glory.

We shared with the nurse that cared for Ayana, affectionately called Lolli, that she was an excited freshman at her father's alma mater, St. Augustine University in Raleigh, North Carolina; a criminal justice major; an active member of the Maryland State Police Explorer Program; a Girl Scout; a debutante; and, that she had played basketball at Largo High School, located not too far from the hospital. We reminisced about all the funny and crazy things that our two daughters had done.

The nurse asked Anthony and I to step out of the room, delayed our return, and then asked to speak to us privately. I knew that it was not good news. When the doctor spoke the words, "I regret to inform you that your daughter has died," I responded, "It's God's will." As I breathed those words, I still experienced the same weird sense of peace that had lingered with me for those 12 hours of waiting. In a few short hours, the news media (local and national), family, and friends would help us share with the masses how special Ayana Jazmyn McAllister was.

The nurse who had cared for Ayana for only five hours began to cry. I comforted him with encouragement from Philippians 4:7. When word spread that Ayana J. McAllister had taken her heavenly flight, family and friends gathered to support us. My sorority sisters went ahead and prepared our home to receive guests who flooded us with love. When I climbed in bed that Tuesday night, I was operating on fumes. Yet, I dared not sleep without time with our God of peace. After prayer and meditation, I fell into a sound sleep and awakened Wednesday morning well rested. I was still experiencing that weird peace, knowing that this was not a dream; our baby was dead! Each night following Ayana's death, there was no struggle to get to sleep. I slept like a baby. Whether in shock or in denial, God was giving me peace in the middle of the biggest storm of my life. Only God could reveal what He was up to with this peace. In retrospect, I know that God used me as an instrument of His will to teach and to be taught through that tragic experience.

An onslaught of local news reporters requested interviews with my husband and I. One evening, supporters gathered to watch one nightly news segment with us. As I watched my husband and I being interviewed, it was surreal. I could not recall that interview at all. As I sat there on the loveseat, watching and listening to Bruce Johnson, the local news anchor, ask us questions, I found myself surprised at my answers. I still could not remember the interview. It's almost as if I were having an out-of-body experience.

At the thought of not remembering, I didn't panic. But I did say quietly, "God, I can't do this!" God reminded me that He had prepared me for such a time as this. As I calmly continued to watch the interview, I heard the anchor, Bruce Johnson, inform the listening audience that the person who killed my daughter had not been caught. He turned to me and said, "Mrs. McAllister, what would you like to say to this person who killed your daughter, if that person is listening?" With tears flowing down my face, I heard my voice speak boldly, "I forgive you! I forgive you for killing my daughter..." I stated that my daughter's homicide was a loss to the community, but it was also a loss for the person who killed her. "No parent should have to bury their child, neither should parents have to visit their children in prison." The entire room seemed to give a collective gasp, then silence prevailed. It looked as if I was watching the remainder of the interview, but I was not. I was in a silent conversation with myself. "I am shocked at you!" I screamed silently to myself. "Forgive? Did you say, 'I forgive the person who killed Ayana.' Your baby?"

As I heard me speaking to myself, I also heard God's still, small voice speaking to me. "From the time you received Daja's call and through twelve hours of waiting to hear the doctor's report, you prayed for your baby to live, but there was no thought of the perpetrator." Truth is, I really had not focused on the perpetrator. The "peace that surpasses all understanding" flooded my mind and my heart. YES, LORD, YES! God had just used me to give the listening world a lesson on forgiveness. This was not my plan, but clearly it was God's.

My loved ones worried that I was too calm. Truth is, I was worried too. Why am I so peaceful? Even though I had my moments of crying, I was still at peace. I still struggle to explain it to others. While I knew Ayana was never coming home, would not return to or graduate from college, get married, or have a family of her own, and there would be no more of her awesome hugs, I had this strange peace. During the same week that Ayana passed, God woke me up early each morning and brought lessons to my memory that I had used with my daughters. I often said to my daughters, "You never have to run away from home. If you find anyone who loves you more than your dad and me, I will take you to them and I will ask them if they have room enough for me, because I want to live with anyone who could love you as much as me." As I reflected on that, God said, "Ayana has a better home, and there is room for you too, but not yet."

Another lesson that came to mind was about borrowed items. "When somebody loans you something, return it with gratefulness." I often shared this lesson with my daughter, Daja, who often borrowed Ayana's things but was challenged with returning the items nicely. God reminded me, Ayana was never mine, but always His. And she was loaned to me for a period of time, to be returned back to Him. At that moment, my mind recalled Ayana and me talking about death after my goddaughter lost her mother while she was in middle school. Ayana said, "Mommy, when you die, I'm going to have to die too because I can't live without you. I explained to Ayana that, "We all belong to God and it's appointed that we shall all die" (Hebrews 9:27). "Ayana," I said, "When it's my time, I want you to live your life. I will be watching you from Heaven. God will take care of you." Never did I realize that that lesson was for me.

God is sovereign and doesn't need our permission to take back what is already His. If God had asked my permission to take my beloved Ayana, I would have replied, "No God, get Yourself another girl." I came to realize that Ayana was God's gift on loan to me and all that loved her. Since Ayana's death, I experience more restful sleep. I have a "peace that surpasses all understanding." While I hurt deeply, I want to be intentional in giving back to God the gift He loaned to us. It's time to say farewell.

I've always thought God had a sense of humor, but this takes the cake. On the day of Ayana's funeral, I was getting dressed and talking to myself, although my husband was in the room. While weeping, I told God I would take bad grades, nasty attitudes, a baby, hell, I'd be ok with twins right now. These things I had cautioned both of my daughters to not bring home, but saying goodbye to my baby was too much. Still weeping and wailing, I yelled to the heavens, "You know I love her! You know I love her." He whispered, "You don't love her more than Me." With that, my tears dried up like the desert. I got dressed and went to bury my baby. The look on my husband's face told me that he was confused. He didn't know what to make of the exchange that happened in front of him but was not with him. He witnessed me talking out loud to myself, crying the entire time only to end suddenly, and then moving on as if nothing had happened. I thought about it months later. Yes, it must have seemed weird. He never asked about it and I never mentioned it.

In my remarks at the funeral, I shared that in spite of this funeral, God is still good. God was good to me before Ayana died and He is still good. We were all in place when the tragedy occurred. Anthony and I celebrated our twenty-fifth anniversary a month earlier out of the country, but He saw fit to have us home together when we got the news. Daja was with Ayana and could give us an accurate account of her last conscious moments. Ayana's guest roommate from Atlanta, Georgia, also was grazed by a bullet. God spared me the guilt of someone else's child being killed while on my watch. Yes, my plans for my life and Ayana's life have been changed, not by choice, but by chance. Even in my sadness, I will bless the Lord at ALL times, His praise shall continually be in my mouth.

God knows the end from the beginning. On the same day the girls arrived home for spring break, we received a letter from the insurance company informing us that we were under a new administration because of a buyout. Usually, my husband would be the keeper of important papers, but for some reason I had put the mail in my purse. Ordinarily, this may not be of importance, but after we were told my daughter had died, the information for her insurance policy was in my purse. God was saying, "I've got this, and I've got Ayana, too."

Oh, the peace I felt watching that beautiful carriage, pulled by two white horses, carrying our baby to her final resting place. Words cannot capture the peace I was feeling because through it all God guarded my heart and mind in Christ Jesus.

I miss Ayana every day, yet I find comfort in knowing that she is with God, who loves her far better than I ever could. Without Ayana, I find it difficult to say that my life is better; but, spiritually I have a closer relationship with God, and I trust God wholeheartedly. I am in tune with Him and when He speaks, I hear Him. It is with a grateful heart that I have been able to forgive the person who killed our precious baby and not be consumed by the fact that the person has not been identified.

SOUL REFLECTION:

Peace is easy to maintain when things are going as planned; however, when you encounter a crisis or your world is falling apart, peace seems unattainable. Our human reasoning supports that grave circumstances call for us to fall apart; however, God can give you a peace that does not seem reasonable or rational. My ability to maintain the peace of God, during and after my child was murdered, has been a great testimony to others who have been troubled. To God be the glory.

Two Is Not Better Than One

LADDA HAWKINS

"Their loyalty is divided between God and the world,
and they are unstable in everything they do."

—James 1:8 (NLT)

The image that comes to my mind of a double-minded man is one of a two-headed monster; something out of Greek mythology. Of course, that wicked abomination would not be a divine creature. Yet, this image is what God is figuratively comparing our actions to in this Scripture. If that is not disturbing enough, consider this. We have all experienced a sleepless night tossing around in bed, going back and forth into sleep, not getting any rest whatsoever. Now, what if I told you that in that back and forth jerking you were actually causing traumatic brain injury? Would that be enough to force you to lie still in the bed? Would that knowledge add to or take away from the frantic activity going on inside of your head? I am surely not a doctor, but I have worked with many people who experienced trauma during my career as a special education teacher and I can assure you restless sleep patterns are not a healthy habit to have. But I want to delve just a little bit deeper and ask, do you consider yourself to be a person who has experienced trauma? In general, trauma can be defined as a psychological or emotional response to an event or an experience that is deeply distressing or disturbing. When loosely applied, this trauma definition can refer to something upsetting, such as being involved in an accident, having an illness or injury, losing a loved one, or going through a divorce.

Unfortunately, many of us have experienced a traumatic event at work. Our transition to the workplace is rarely a smooth one, even with years of specialized training. How else can we expect to adjust emotionally if there is little preparation because of how much workplaces vary in structure and support? Funny how we rarely look in the mirror thinking about the image we might bring to the forefront of someone else's mind.

My aim is to help people adjust to workplace induced trauma. My qualifications are cemented in old fashioned experience, although I have invested a large amount of time and resources into my own personal development in the field. My story began when I started to notice how unhappy and depressed I became from not feeling connected to my work and the skills I brought to the workplace. At the time, I was only motivated by money, so I sought out positions in sales to bolster my sensitive ego. I had a nonexistent relationship with God but experienced His grace and mercy through my success which was validated in the field. The Lord had gifted me with discernment at an early age, although I didn't understand how to use this ability to understand a person's needs without their articulation. I just felt it was more of a lucky hunch. However, this high sensitivity had its drawbacks. I found that I easily absorbed emotion and was susceptible to depression when overwhelmed. At first, the roller coaster provided a bit of an adrenaline rush. But trips down the trenches started taking longer and longer to recover from.

One of those dark times just a few hours before dawn, I remember having a violent and sleepless night. My mind was troubled with questions such as why am I here? Does work really matter? Does life even matter anymore? It was in that still of the night that I recall audibly hearing the voice of God speak to me for one of the first times in my adult life. The voice sounded like a soft-spoken male whispering one word... "Help." The tone was reassuring and not distressed. He was not asking for help but offering help. Yes, I need help, o' Lord! But I don't even know how to start, what do I say or do? All I knew to do was to repeat what I heard. So, I let out a similarly soft cry. I repeated the word help. However, my version was saturated with desperation. I simply closed my eyes and waited. I waited with the utmost expectation that my simple request would be heard. Honestly, I wanted an easy way out. My soul was tired and cried for eternal sleep. I wanted to rest. But as I lay with my eyes closed, I finally felt something different. I felt a subtle surrender take place. It felt like the kind of peace you feel after a long, hard cry. My mind stopped racing long enough that I was able to get rest for the morning. However, I knew something had changed for the better that very moment.

Typically, I am a morning person. But, when I was in the depth of my depression, I resented the bright rays of light that peeked from my window. I love positioning my bed to look outside of the window. No matter the view. I felt it was important to rise up each morning in a forward direction. Any other arrangement did not seem to support this feeling. So, as I awoke that morning feeling rested after nearly a month without such a reprieve, I wanted to talk to someone about my experience. As I arrived at work, I had an opportunity to sit with an instructor. We had rarely spoken more than a friendly hello when we passed each other in the hall, but that day it seemed as if she was waiting for me. So, as we were in the campus break room, she initiated a casual conversation which came at the perfect time for me. As we shared extensively, she told me about a counselor that accepted our insurance. I never even knew that mental health counseling was covered by health insurance. In my mind, mental health existed in the form of psychiatric wards as seen on television. I was glad to know no straitjackets with straps would be used in real life.

Later that morning, I called the counseling office to make an appointment. The receptionist kept pushing for me to give her the reason for my call. I felt so embarrassed to have to tell her I needed to talk with someone. She then asked a question that made me want to hang up the phone. She asked, "Are you now or have you recently had suicidal ideations?" I knew this was a bad idea. As I stood holding the phone at work wondering how to best answer this question in front of my now staring coworkers, I whispered, "I don't know." I guess that was the wrong thing to say as her tone quickly changed and I was told to hold for further assistance. That was extremely awkward and uncomfortable. It was becoming too much of a burden. I wondered,

Why am I doing this again? As the receiver started to near the handset, I heard a soft-spoken male voice on the line saying, "Hello, Ladda, I can help." My heart stopped in place. I quickly brought the receiver back closer to my ear, not yet brave enough to utter a sound. The man on the other end repeated his statement. This time the only words that could surpass the growing lump in my throat were, "I am here." We continued to keep the weekly meeting. Surrendering felt natural.

Therapy was similar to attending a class. An agenda was laid out, homework was assigned, and an authoritative figure told me how things were supposed to go. I'm not saying it was a bad thing; however, it was far from a solution to fix the void I still felt within. The greatest benefit of therapy was understanding the need to have a focal point when addressing one issue at a time and how to articulate uncertainty with choice words. My therapist recommended creating a toolbox of strategies during those sessions. Expectations were set for therapy to be a short-term fix, so I needed to make the most of the time. I think if he had not prepared me in that way, I would not have acclimated as quickly. My therapist assigned tons of reading material from various sources including the Bible. As I mentioned earlier, I did not have a relationship with God and knew very little about the Bible. The articles he shared told the biblical stories in a very relatable manner. Those biblical commentaries had discussion questions and piqued my interest in God. I invested in my own copy of T.D. Jakes' Woman, Thou Art Loosed after I discovered this genre of gospel storytelling which seemed to know exactly what I was going through.

Work seemed to become more tolerable as well. Things didn't seem as random anymore. Tasks became opportunities even when no one else volunteered to do them. So, I started to invest in personal development courses, books, and materials. Former interests in leadership development started to reemerge. My friends and coworkers gave me the nickname Google because of my range of curiosities. I liked it, but I had to caution myself on trying to fix others' issues instead of being a source of information. I'm sure Google was never offended that someone did not follow through after a topic search. Why did I feel this way?

Self-reflection is a difficult task. Although I became disciplined in making consistent journal entries, thanks to my therapy toolkit, those entries did not seem genuine. I was not being true to myself. Luckily, this was a time way before social media; but, looking back at the quality of the text, my journal could have easily been published. Sadly, I would not have recognized it as being my own. I was playing it safe. Short-term memory loss is a common characteristic of someone with a traumatic brain injury. The ability to recall what just occurred becomes glossed over with the evidence of what happened right before you. The human brain tries to make it all make sense. My mind wanted to follow the rules of what I was supposed to do, but my spirit was aimless. I was unstable in my ways. It showed because I was still only at a basic self-preservation level. You may have heard that referred to as being concerned with "your core and no more." It was harvesttime after all. Things were going good in my life. I was married with one son, a churchgoer, homeowner, college graduate, and business owner. Why did it still feel like something was missing? God's plan is to orchestrate our steps, one by one. Little did I know at the time that I would be willing to trade in most of the material things and statuses to go with Him to the next level.

This next part of the story runs close to the present day. However, we will start in 2009. I was pregnant with my second child. My marriage was starting to struggle because I was feeling the urge towards more. I wanted to move to Texas. My husband didn't feel there was a reason to venture out West because we had what we wanted in Louisiana—a house, a business, and our immediate families within the Shreveport community. The appeal of moving for more opportunity got stronger with each day. I had recently completed a Texas-based teacher certification program online and needed to fulfill my internship hours. I had to do those hours any way, but I was ready to make the case with every opportunity I could.

Additionally, my maternal instincts were in overdrive during my entire pregnancy. My oldest son was nine years old but having a sibling for him seemed to provide a sense of completion for me. Micheal was born in 2010. The urge to keep pushing became more intense. Daily prayers for direction were answered with blaring confirmation to keep pressing. However, my sense of duty turned quickly to guilt and shame. It was evident that if I wanted more, I would have to leave my comfort zone. Literally, leave my home. My heart was now double-minded and unstable. Have you ever tried to do an emotionally based pros and cons list? How did that work for you? If it was anything like mine, each pro becomes a con and vice versa. Items are not fairly weighted emotionally. There are deal breakers that being aware of from the beginning will help to fairly balance your considerations. This may be the most controversial statement in my story, but I felt God's hand pushed me out of my marriage. If I stayed, it would have been doing so out of fear and not thinking about the benefits to my children. Arguably, raising two young men without a father in the household may not seem like a benefit but looking back over the past nine years, I don't regret a thing. Single parenthood has softened my heart towards others who take risks for the protection and expectation of better things for their children. God's new purpose and spiritual gift for my life is the ministry of reconciliation. For each thing I had been separated from—work, friends, faith, and family—God has restored. The fruit of the Spirit (which is love, joy, peace, forbearance, kindness, faithfulness, gentleness, and self-control) bloomed from the seeds planted when I understood the full circle of life. No longer am I divided between the world and kingdom living when I remember how HE lives within. There is no separation. For each mistake, He offers correction not condemnation. His mercy is undeserved. I felt the calling to nurture the community starting with its women and children. My testimony can be used to let single working parents know that everyday life can and will work out if we remain focused and ask for help.

SOUL REFLECTION:

When the world tells us success comes from the accumulation of many things, God only wants one thing—you! Simply and wonderfully created with a purpose, God wants a relationship with you from the inside out. Your thoughts and actions honor Him. Your work is an expression of this praise. If we lose focus on God, our spirit immediately knows. It will tell you with a gentle voice or insatiable desire for more. The best part of Christian living is that the pathway is forever open and encourages others to join you on the journey.

God's Love: The Gift That Keeps on Giving

ANGELA T. KINNEL

"For God so loved the world, that he gave his only begotten Son, that whosoever believeth in him should not perish, but have everlasting life."

—John 3:16 (KJV)

L-O-V-E... we use this word in so many ways in our everyday lives. We tell those who we think are most important to us that we love them. We fall in love with a significant other and at some point say, "I love you" with no hesitation. We use the word love to describe how we feel about songs, food, movies, clothes, sports teams, schools, restaurants, and pictures. But the question of whether we really know what love is continues to arise in my mind. As believers we say and feel that God loves us. But do we really know what the love of God truly involves? While I'm sure that I've had the answer in more ways than one, I was awakened to His love for me after receiving Him in my heart and changing my mindset of what love really involved.

The Merriam-Webster dictionary defines love as a: *(1) strong affection for another arising out of kinship or personal* ties *(maternal love for a child)*, *(2) attraction based on sexual desire: affection and tenderness felt by lovers, (3) affection based on admiration, benevolence, or common interests (love for his old schoolmates)*. As you can see, love has many meanings as a noun, verb, and an adjective. However, there are four different types of love from the Greek language: eros, phileo, storge, and agape. Eros is a passionate and intense love that arouses romantic feelings. It focuses more on self than the other person. It looks for what it can receive. If it does give, it gives in order to receive. Phileo is an affectionate, warm, and tender platonic love. It makes you desire friendship with someone. It responds to appreciation and kindness. It involves giving as well as receiving but can collapse in a crisis. Storge is a kind of family and friendship love. It's the love that parents feel naturally for their children. The love that members of a family have for each other. Lastly, agape is the noblest word for love. It is a chosen and committed type of love. It is unconditional and sees beyond the surface and accepts the person for who he or she is, regardless of faults. This love delights in giving. This is the love that God has for you and me! Agape love is the love of God. God is love!

To be loved by God is a pure gift given to the undeserving and the unlovable. We can't provoke, trick, convince, earn, or win love from God. It is a love that finds its ultimate definition in the cross of Jesus Christ, where the innocent Son of God takes the place of the guilty. In the Mirror Bible, 1 John 4:7-11 plainly describes the love God has for us:

[7] "Beloved, love always includes others, since love springs from God; its source is found in the fellowship of the Father,

Son, and the Holy Spirit. Everyone who encounters love immediately knows that they too are born of the same source! It is not possible to fully participate in love without discovering God. To love is to know God; to know God is to love.

8 Not to love, is not to know God. There is nothing in love that distracts from who God is. Love is who God is — they are inseparable.

9 The love of God is unveiled within us in the Son; He was begotten of the Father in the flesh and sent into the world that we might live because of Him. Our lives are mirrored and defined in Him. Both His birth in the flesh as well as His commission into the world were entirely God's doing.

10 Love is not defined by our love for God, but by His love for us! It is not our response to God that attracts His attention; we have always had His undivided affection as declared in the prophetic promise and finally demonstrated in His Son's commission and work of atonement for our sins.

11 Loved Ones! If this is true about God's love for us, it is equally true of His love in us for others!"

This is a gift like no other! This is what's available to each of us if we believe on Him. To have His undivided affection ALL the time is a blessing. Receiving God's love in my life allowed me to understand who I truly was. As described in John 3:16, He thought you and I were to die for! Do you know anybody that's willing to do that for you? God sent His only begotten Son so that we may live eternally in Him. Jesus shares the same Divine nature as God as opposed to us (believers) who are God's sons and daughters by adoption. Jesus is God's "one and only" Son. That same love led Jesus to the cross. He gave Himself for us in order to redeem us from the curse of the law. We have the same identity as Christ! It's in our DNA!

If we all received this, we as the body of Christ would be united. Being united in the eyes of the Lord blesses Him and serves hell a mighty blow. We must be courageous and fearless while going about the business of God because we have legions of angels guarding us. We also have two friends that stay within close proximity of us. Their names are goodness and mercy! They follow us all the days of our lives! We are in great company!

How amazing is the love of God! In 1 John 3:1 it says that we should look at how great a love the Father has given us, that we should be called God's children. No one can harm us nor remove us from His hands. He will never leave us nor forsake us. We are children of the most high God! We are saved by grace through faith and qualified! We are free to love ourselves and others. God loves us with an everlasting love. He can't stop loving us. He didn't have to think about it and make up His mind about loving us.

I want to share with you eight benefits that we as believers have due to God's love for us:

1.   We were chosen before the creation of the world. (Ephesians 1:4, 11)
2.   We belong to God. We were bought with a price (purchased with a preciousness and paid for, made His own. (1 Corinthians 6:20, AMP)
3.   We are justified. We are justified (acquitted, declared righteous, and given right standing with God) through faith. (Romans 5:1, AMP)

4. We are established, anointed, and sealed by God. (2 Corinthians 1:21-22)
5. We are citizens of Heaven. (Philippians 3:20)
6. We are holy and blameless. (Ephesians 1:4)
7. We are hidden in Christ with God. (Colossians 3:3)
8. We are dwellings for the Holy Spirit. (Ephesians 2:22)

SOUL REFLECTION:
Taking hold of the benefits available to us all gave me clarity of who I am in Christ. I know that no matter what my past looked like, God still loved me with no conditions. I gained a lot of confidence from that. Understanding the love of God and the gifts as a result of it has allowed me to walk in love with those who aren't lovable. It has given me the courage to stand firm in who I am in Him and who He has called me to be.

The Shift: Knowing When to Move

CRYSTAL CUNNINGHAM

*"Trust in the Lord with all thine heart; and lean not unto
thine own understanding. In all thy ways acknowledge
him, and he shall direct they paths."*

—Proverbs 3:5-6 (KJV)

When God asks you to trust Him, you do. Trusting was not easy for me; I have been disappointed by so many people that trust has become one of the hardest things for me to do. Many promises have been made only to be broken. So, when the nudging and whisper came that God would be releasing me from my job, I fought the process. I tried to move the mountain in my own strength which only made matters worse.

When God was unveiling His plan to me about moving into ministry and becoming a small business owner, I struggled with it. My background did not match up to the assignment. So, I know how you feel about letting go of your safety net and fully giving into God's will. *Here I am at this great company going on 19 plus years and You want me to do what? Leave.* No... that could not be the will of God.

However, three years prior, I was facing a really difficult time in my life. It seemed as if my world was crumbling right before my eyes. My mind was being tormented by the enemy and I found myself secretly hopeless. Once again, I put back on the mask of covering up the pain and confusion that sat with me day after day. It wasn't until one particular week that it really felt as if the doors and walls were closing in on me. I was getting little sleep, if any, at times. I would find myself up in the middle of the night pacing or crying, trying to figure out how I would get myself out of this web I was in. I happened to go into the office one day earlier than my normal time, so it was just me sitting at the desk. I believe the quietness drew me in and I started to experience my first panic attack. My manager decided on that same day to come in early and saw me breaking down at my desk. She immediately removed me from the call I was on and recommended that I go home. I called my Employee Assistance Program and they started the process of me getting some therapy. Yes, the minister needed to resolve some hidden fears that had been lying dormant. One day while I was at home, I took my Word out and started reading and praying. Then, on one beautiful spring morning while in prayer, for the first time ever I heard an audible voice speak to me. This voice was different. If you are wondering, we all hear a voice. It can be our conscience, subconscious (this is where the enemy will reside), or the voice of the Lord.

It was the Spirit Himself talking directly to me. The words that I heard changed my life! I heard, "Healing has just stepped out of Heaven," and then there was an image to go along with it. It was as big as a slab of concrete on the sidewalk. What I was discerning was the word abundance. Everything was going to be alright. In addition, I heard, "I know the plans that I have for you, Crystal, they are of good and not of evil, to give you peace and an expected end. Do not be afraid when I take you off the job." The peace that came upon me was nothing I had ever experienced. Afterwards, there were specific instructions on how to start praying and fasting. Even though I was told those things, the internal warfare did not cease. That's when the real work began for me in order for my lifestyle to change. I struggled with believing that anything good would happen for me without me making it happen. To put my total trust in God was hard, but I understood that if I was going to come out of that moment alive and in my right mind, I would have to surrender my will for His will. I had to cut loose some of the things I was involved in. I did not realize that I had switched roles and become an enabler to someone's wrong behavior. BUT GOD! He knows all things and He is a forgiving God. I repented and started the process to let go and move forward.

I went back to asking God about His statement, "Do not be afraid when I take you off the job." I asked Him, "Wait, I'm leaving? It wasn't like I did not know one day that I would exit my company doors, but to do what I think You are calling me to do is another challenge. Ministry in the marketplace, what is that? Take Your Word and do what with who?" All types of questions ran across my mind. I had stopped doing the empowerment workshops, monthly forums, and outreach work. I thought I was done. I was okay attending conferences and listening to other people speak and share their stories. "You want me to publicly tell my story to who? Where? When?" I was led by the Holy Spirit to start a Facebook Live—giving out the Word, asking people if they needed prayer, and telling my story. Little did I know God was setting me up for the calling He placed on my life. So, even though I was afraid to talk in front of the camera as an adult, I remembered that I was never shy or afraid as a young girl. My father and my family would call on me to dance or sing with the adults. What happened? I discovered I was robbed of my confidence earlier on in life. Through various experiences, my voice was stolen, and my vulnerability, identity, confidence, and trust in people were all taken. I had learned to become very guarded and not let anyone in. To constantly go through the hurt, betrayal, lies, manipulation, and disappointment was too much. The disappointment was the hardest. I felt that at an early age I was disappointed a lot due to promises made by my family members that were not kept. I had to learn to trust God.

I remember one day while riding down the highway, He revealed to me that I did not trust Him. I could not allow God to have complete control. I did that before with my husband, and that did not turn out well for me. I carried the burden of shame for years because I trusted in what he said. How did I know that God would not shame me? How could I trust God? The Bible says, "God is not a man, so he does not lie." Numbers 23:19 (NLT). When this passage of Scripture came back to my memory, I knew I was either going to believe what I read and heard, or I was not. That is how what I call Midnight Ministry began. Just about every night, I started to go live and what I realized was that people would actually join the broadcast. God told me that people are looking for a solution to their problem and His Word provides exactly that, a solution to everything. In the midnight hour is when the enemy will torment God's people the most. The audience grew and so did my confidence to tell my story and share the Word. I was talked about during those times because people thought I was crazy for coming on at that time and delivering the Word. Little did I know that would be the catalyst to the main thing.

I kept hearing in my spirit, "Go scout out the land." Because I had given God a yes early on, He wanted it back. During that time, I started to discern that God wanted me to go and check out Texas to become my new location. Your faith will always be tested and tried, and your obedience is the determining factor if you will past the test. At that time, I had only been to Texas twice, once for Mega Fest and once for Woman Thou Art Loosed with Bishop T.D. Jakes. The very first time I went to Texas, I turned my phone on while coming out of the airport and my girlfriend sent me a text message asking if I could see myself living there. I took a double take at the phone, looked around the area and responded, "NO!" I did not like it. There was too much open space; it felt just like a desert. Did she forget that we are from New York with lots of people and very tall buildings? I was hearing crickets. No, this was not the place for your girl. LOL. In the back of my mind, I wondered why she asked me that. A few years would pass by but that little "Do not be afraid when I take you off the job" voice still whispered in my ear. By that time, I started to become uncomfortable at my job. And when I was led to scout out the land, I went back to Texas. Not knowing exactly where to go, I prayed and fasted, seeking God's face. The only thing I heard was Galleria. So, I went to Google (thank God for some Google) and located the area in Dallas. I made my flight and hotel reservations and left to go scout it out. I arrived in the late evening only to realize that I had gone there before for the conference. Everything was in one location and I was not venturing out, not at first anyway. After my second trip, I did, and that's when I started to get in alignment even more. I had mapped out a few apartments to go look at but none of them were really to my liking.

I went back to the hotel, got in the bed, and put the covers over my head. I wanted to hide. I must have been wrong. Did I really hear from God? The next morning, I heard, "You have come too far, and faith requires action." I jumped out of the bed, started to praise and pray, and immediately I felt strengthened. By that time, I was riding through Dallas like a pro, knowing where to turn and of course you know I found the mall. What woman goes to a new state and does not know where the mall or shopping outlets are? The day was coming to an end and there was one particular place that I wanted to see, Uptown. That part of town was everything I had imagined for myself. But I was too late. The leasing office was closing up for the day, so I was not able to get a tour of the apartments, but I did take a tour of the grounds. They were absolutely beautiful.

Upon returning home, the fear of the unknown started and I knew that I would have to increase my time in the Word and fasting. See, what I noticed was that when I continually stayed in that secret place God talks about, I was able to keep my peace. The battle of provision became my issue.

And to be honest, having more than enough or just enough was always the issue. I was used to surviving not thriving and living the abundant life. Today, Midnight Ministry is flourishing along with my speaking engagements and coaching practice. Not in a million years would I think of myself as an author, but as of now I have released two books, *Rise Up in Hope* and *Soulful Prayers*.

SOUL REFLECTION:
After a long time of waiting and almost moving ahead of God, the time eventually came just like He said it would. My courage was stronger, and my belief was elevated beyond measure. On September 14, 2018, Hurricane Florence surfaced sending me out of my house for over 14 days. I had to escape back to New York. The morning I was set to start my journey back home, I received a message that Verizon Wireless was offering their employees a separation package. On that same morning, I was awakened by a whisper of where my new home would be. It was all coming together. After a 19-year career with one of the world's top telecommunications companies, the cord of that long-term relationship was cut on March 22, 2019. I walked out the door with more than I had when I first stepped into Bell Atlantic Mobile 19 years prior. God used my job to reveal the gift that was hidden in this treasure box.

Trust what God has spoken to you and in His timing things will come to pass. What the enemy wants to do is frustrate you, distract you, tempt you, and lead you in the wrong direction. But what you are discerning is more than likely true—there is more to your life. Know when to let go and take the leap, for we walk by faith, not by sight. (2 Corinthians 5:7, CSB)

God Is My Husband

JACQUELINE L. SHAW

"Be still, and know that I am God."

—Psalm 46:10 (NKJV)

In my adult years, I had long sensed and experienced God being right beside me. This was through experiences, tears of joy and pain, and times of moaning and praying. My personal experience with Him was so great, but to a certain extent I really didn't know how great of an experience it was. Nor did I convey this to my children. The not so funny thing was I didn't understand what the Bible was saying.

Little did I know that I was not paying full attention to the red lines of writing being God the Son speaking in His wisdom. I was just reading along with others in church or in Bible Study without true attentiveness. Imagine, every week my three beautiful daughters and I would pick up our individual Bible's on Sunday before heading out the door like clockwork. Also, like clockwork, we would return home, place the Bible's in their respective spots, only to repeat the process every Sunday. This regimen was about to be changed as I was not prepared for the moment when something was about to go wrong.

I've been consistent in my career and not had the need to change to other ventures. I love what I do and have also engaged my daughters whenever there was a need. They even volunteer to assist when they are available. Early in their lives, as they entered college and came home for breaks, I would employ them. My husband was in Human Resources as a director. There came a time when he switched companies. We had discussed the new opportunity and was anxious for another beginning in his growth as he became a VP. Not much time had passed before we were attending our very first Christmas party with his new associates.

We were having a good time at the party and I got to meet the CEO of the company. He basically made an appearance and left early. The party continued and then the strangeness began. I didn't know what to think because of the happenings going on. It became clear to me that the new people my husband was working with had very different lifestyles than ours. Let's just say it didn't matter whether you were married or single or who you came with. "Be a willing participant" was the motto.

The longer my husband worked for that new company, the more he adapted to the lifestyle of his co-workers. At home he had the suburban Huxtable's lifestyle, but he also adopted this wild side where he would frequent night clubs until 2:00 a.m. One time after a night out, he lost his wedding band (or so he said). With much badgering, he confessed he had taken it off to dance with other women. All of that was unimaginable. After many disagreements, feelings of sadness and rejection, and his refusal to give up his acquired lifestyle, I knew that in time a divorce was imminent. I wanted to reflect only on the best of times, this marriage was supposed to be a dream come true.

While going through a difficult time over the matter of infidelity, I reached out to one of my good friends who was a prayer warrior at my church. Let's just call her P.W. There was something different about her that attracted me to her. She had a peace and grace about herself. I wanted to be just like that. It had to be a wonderful feeling because she seemed so awesome to me. She was extremely supportive of my plight as were several other friends. This was a part of what they were there for, right?

I was married to my husband for seventeen years. We would experience a rough patch every so often, as most if not all marriages do. In the seventeenth year, here's where the unthinkable happened. There were no warning signs nor hints of what was to come.

When we said our wedding vows, I literally took to heart the "for better, for worse, for richer, for poorer, in sickness and in health, to love and to cherish" as a model for how the rest of life was to be with this man. He was a year older than me. We were worlds apart as I was in one state and he was in another. How we came to know each other was through cousins of mine; his parents lived three houses down from them. Of course, in those early years, we weren't thinking about life situations. He was like one of the family. We went through many years—elementary, junior high, and high school—still knowing of each other. At age 21, most people are looking forward to being the legal age so that they can experience the club life. I experienced going to the state where he was, us seeing each other, me thinking he was the most handsome man I had ever seen, and him thinking I was the most beautiful woman. From there, we dated for a short period of time long distance. We were making trips almost every weekend with him coming to where I was or me going to where he was. I recall he even drove through a thunderstorm to get to where I was. Young love!

Eventually that became too much, and he convinced me it was time to move to where he was. Following my heart, I did that very thing. Not long after, we were in wedded bliss. Genesis 2:24 says, "For this reason a man shall leave his father and his mother, and be joined to his wife, and they shall become one flesh." Our daughters were all born three years apart in the same city. Later, we moved to a different city to start life afresh. I didn't want to experience or touch on divorce, but it became a reality within a year of meeting his new acquaintances.

Eventually the divorce did occur, and it felt like being ripped into slowly. I wasn't sleeping and it was very hard holding it together for my girls. I guess this is where that glorious phrase from Proverbs 3:5—"Trust in the Lord with all your heart and lean not on your own understanding"— comes into play. The pain, the anger, and the hurting feelings I was having were beginning to be too much for me. But GOD began speaking to me, telling me to just "be still and know that I am God," because I had so many negative words and thoughts building up within me. He warned me that "death and life are in the power of the tongue." I was not my usual self. At the time, I didn't know that phrase was in the Bible, but I knew they were words from God. I stopped arguing with my husband because God continued speaking to me.

I began praying more, studying, and talking to God daily. I asked God to fill me with His Holy Spirit constantly.

It seemed like a slow process, but after a few months I realized I had the qualities of peace and grace that I had recognized in my friend the prayer warrior. I believed they were gifts from the Holy Spirit. I would still have some moments of controllable anger. One day while at the bank, I felt indignant about his waywardness. I thought, *The nerve of him not wanting me! I'm beautiful! I'm an entrepreneur with my own business for multiple years! I thought I was his forever until the end woman! What man wouldn't want me?* Then it dawned on me, I have a husband; I have God! I left the bank and as I was sitting in my car, I began praising His name out loud with "Lord, I thank you!" I'm sure everyone who passed by was wondering about my sanity. That day it finally hit me that God took care of my needs and my children's needs as well.

I understood that God was in fact the perfect husband.

As time moved on, the girls were introduced to seven different women within a year. I wasn't too sure what my ex-husband's thought process was then. In my opinion, it surely wasn't a good reflection of how a man should carry himself, much less how disrespectful it was to our girls. You know what I mean? It was like a different parade after each corner was turned. Still I prayed for him to become better and to get to a point of being active in church and turning from those ways. One Sunday, I had been informed that he was at the church I attended. Ok, it was somewhat of a good thing that he was attending church somewhere. Before, he barely attended any service mostly because he wanted to travel a distance that was not conducive to me getting the three girls and myself ready in a timely manner. I learned later that a woman I thought was my friend (let's call her W.H.), someone who attended women's Bible study with me as well as whom I asked to pray for my marriage while experiencing the tough time, was not who I thought she was. You all know where I'm going with this right? You know the saying, "Be careful who you ask to pray for you." My confidence was obviously not confidential and respected as she ended up dating him.

So, get this, my ex started coming to church regularly, even going to Sunday School with her and to a class that was across the hall from mine. That was the hardest thing my daughters and I went through. Watching him show a loving interest in someone else and her children. Children that were younger than his own daughters. Yes, I prayed for him to do better; but, of all the churches in Texas, he had to choose the very one I was attending. Oh, you can believe I had some choice words for them both. But God said to be still and know that I am God. Hold your tongue. Death and life are in the power of the tongue. Choose life.

My conversation with God was, "Do you see what I'm going through? Do you see what this man is doing? He is saying terrible things about me to make himself look better. God, you just want me to be quiet and not defend myself?" Once again, God said, "Be still and know that I am God. I will fight your battle for you."

My stubbornness had me hating going to church every Sunday if he was there. But God said I had to go. I was even beginning to say that I hated my ex-husband with a passion.

Proverbs 10:12 says, "Hatred stirs up conflict, but love covers all wrongs." I was not displaying the right attitude as Scripture suggests.

Ironically, my ex left the church and got married, but not to the one whom I had trusted and he was dating. God truly doesn't like ugly!

As for the one he did marry, if I had the ability to pick a step-mother for my girls, I would say she fit the mold. She's kind, caring, thoughtful, and a great role model for any young lady. Look at God!

SOUL REFLECTION:
Before my divorce, I thought I had a relationship with God. Now, after everything I have been through, I can truly say that I have an intimate, personal relationship with God. I always remind myself that people will let me down, they will try to hurt me, and they may disappoint me, but I will not let the actions of others block my relationship with the Father by holding unforgiveness. Instead, I choose to forgive so that I can increase my capacity to receive everything He has in store for me!

I Faint Not...

LASONJA S. CAMPBELL

"Trust in the Lord with all of thine heart; and lean not unto thine own understanding. In all thy ways acknowledge him, and he shall direct thy paths."

—Proverbs 3:5-6

Tick-tock, tick-tock, my biological clock was ticking. I could hear it. It was clear that at the age of forty, my dream of having children was disappearing. Sadly, I would not have children and the chance of falling in love and finding "Mr. Right" was also fading quickly.

Growing up in Flint, Michigan, I've always been rooted in the church, present in Sunday school, singing in the choir, and actively participating in most activities. A fairly attractive girl with a cola bottle shape, I typically captured the eyes of older boys, and unfortunately, older men. In fact, I often felt very uncomfortable and could feel their eyes undressing me on many occasions.

One typical fall morning, I dressed myself, ate a bowl of cereal, and left my home as a bubbly seventh grader headed to middle school. I left the Suburban Court cul-de-sac and headed up a long street called Gracelawn. My walk to school was about 25 minutes and I generally walked alone. About 10 minutes into the walk, I could sense that someone was behind me. Should I turn around? Should I look? The footsteps seemed to get louder and faster. I turned and I looked. It was a man. His face was covered with a black stocking cap and I literally peed my pants. All I could do was scream. I took off running in the street, then I ran across the street while screaming bloody murder. I did not even think as my instinct was to return to the safest space I knew. I ran home. I am not exactly sure why I was wearing slippers, but I kicked them off to run. It seemed like I was running for hours before I made it to the side door of our home. I am not sure why he stopped chasing me or when he stopped but he did. It was my first bad encounter with men, but not my last.

I spent the next few days, weeks, and months trying to forget "the day that I was almost raped." Working hard to forget the masked man. Working to bury my feelings of hurt and disbelief. There were several bad encounters. Older boys looked at me and even touched me. I spent many years suffering in silence, and I asked the age-old question, why me?

It was a few years later when I learned that my birth father was going to prison. It was a very sad day, but I pretended it did not matter. I don't know whose child my father touched, but I was embarrassed that it happened. I was so afraid that one day my friends would find out. In the back of my mind, I knew that it was bad because when I was about two my father killed my godfather and did not spend any time in prison. So, the fact that he was now going to prison after this crime meant it was bad, very bad. There are still a lot of unknowns and unanswered questions, but just like the man that almost raped me and the older boys that touched me, my goal was to bury those feelings deep inside. I had to hide the pain, bury the embarrassment, and simply keep it movin'.

In 1986, I graduated from Flint Northwestern High School and made my way to the highest of seven hills in Tallahassee, Florida, to attend Florida Agricultural and Mechanical University (FAMU). That was my chance to start over and begin my new life. But as you might expect, my problems with men worsened. I was more comfortable with my body, but the "S curves" were real. Although I had a steady boyfriend for most of my years in college, we broke up. It was during that time that I slept in my room and was awakened to someone in my bed. I was told, "Keep quiet and do not yell." With his hand firmly over my mouth it happened. I couldn't run down the street to my safe space. I could not make it to my mom. I was stuck. He raped me. He left. I lay in my bed crying. I was horrified. I knew him; I know him. It was my fault. I deserved it. I had learned from an early age that when bad things happen, it's important to bottle up the feelings, store them away, and put them on a shelf. Unfortunately, when the wind blows (in this case, being raped by someone I knew; a casual acquaintance) it disrupts everything. I had dodged this bullet so many times, how could this happen to me? Why even ask why? It was too early to ask because things would get worse.

A few weeks later, I headed home from college for the summer. I was excited for a change of scenery and I was headed to my safe space. I arrived but could not seem to bounce back. I was sad. I was moping around and had really started falling into deep despair. I wanted to die. I could not understand why God would allow that to happen to me. I had been faithful. I was not perfect, but I served Him throughout my life and always found ways to give Him all the glory. But I could not seem to shake how I was feeling. My get up and go had gotten up and gone. After a couple of weeks of moping and laying around the house, my mom took me to the doctor.

Oh my God! What? Pregnant?!!! This could not be happening. I thought the night of the rape was the worst day of my life—nope, this was it! I cried. The pain of the almost rape, being touched by boys, the rape, and now this. I didn't want a baby. Besides, if I wanted a baby, I could have had one. I want a husband and a family, not some bastard child (my thinking at the time) that was conceived during a rape. I thought, *How could I let this happen? Lord, why me? What am I going to do?*

I am a scholar and I spent my entire life focused on graduating from college and defying the stereotypes of an inner-city black girl. Now, my life was going to be different. I cannot remember if my mom asked me what I wanted to do. I think she did, but I knew that I did not want a baby. My mom and I never really discussed the rape in much detail, and I believe that she may have thought it was a cover-up for mischievous behavior as a college girl. Either way, that baby was not entering the world.

My PHAT (pretty hips, a$$, and thighs) body has been a curse in some ways. It's come with some very unwanted attention from men. For years, I've internalized the pain and found it difficult to have relationships with men. I am now 40, with no babies and no man. I've longed to be a mother and a wife. I determined that my bad decisions, unfortunate circumstance, and bad genes would be the reasons why I would never have my dreams fulfilled and live "the Huxtable life." Waking up in the middle of the night with a heavy heart, I felt broken and so alone. Many nights I cried myself to sleep, only to awaken in fear. Reliving all of it... everything. I would simply sit up in the pitch darkness and literally reach my hand to the heavens and pray, "Father, I stretch my hand to thee, no other help do I know!" Night after night that was my ritual. Cry, sleep, wake, cry, pray, repeat.

But then finally one night God answered, "Delight yourself in the Lord and He will grant you the desires of your heart" (Psalm 37:4). My desire was to have a husband and some babies, but time was running out on both. I listened to a sermon and the prophetess suggested that we needed to stop asking God to send us a saved husband if we were not prepared as a saved wife. It was time for me to really focus on and do what God wanted me to do.

The first thing that I had to do was stop blaming myself for all the negative encounters with men. As a strong black woman, I had to admit that I was a victim from a young age; it was not my fault. I did not ask for those things to occur and most importantly I did not deserve them, none of them. Then, I had to forgive each of the men who wronged me; my life depended on it. If I truly wanted God to bless me, it was important that I lived a life of purity although I was no longer a virgin. I did that. I practiced abstinence for years, I was committed to pleasing God.

In 2009, I was attending Triumph Church in Detroit, Michigan, and serving on The Leadership Institute ministry.

I was assigned to teach a class with a man from the church. The hours of preparation and conversation eventually led to us engaging socially and hanging out. I thought he was attractive, but I was already in a relationship with God. In fact, my mantra was "Singleness is a whole number." I was open to love, but my priority was ensuring that I was everything God wanted me to be and then some!

So, with playing matchmaker in mind, I began to ask the man from the church a lot of questions to best understand his character. He was such an awesome man of God I thought, *I am going to hook this guy up with one of my good girl friends*. My plan, however, would be short circuited when I told "Ms. Perspective." Ms. Perspective responded with a real sister girl question, "Do you have a man? If not, then hook your darn self up!" Yes, my girl said it... with a few choicer words! I had an immediate aha moment and hung up my matchmaking hat no sooner than I had put it on. As time progressed, the man from the church and I would visit regularly and develop a true friendship. We soon found ourselves increasingly attracted to one another.

After a year, we began to talk about being a couple. My alone time with God allowed me to prepare and gain clarity on a few things. First, my definition of dating. I defined dating as getting to know what you like and dislike by going out with multiple people (A, B, C, and D) versus knowing what you like and *still* toggling between A and B. I clearly communicated that I would not be in a relationship with anyone in which I was one of two women. During my quiet time with God, I also identified my non-negotiables in a relationship. They were simple and any man that I dated could not violate any of them. No ifs, ands, or buts. Here were my must haves in a relationship with a man:

1. God-fearing man — Someone who has a relationship with God and understands that failure to respect me as a saved woman of God is punishable by our Father.

2. Someone who is fiscally responsible — Not rich but makes good financial decisions.

3. A great communicator — Someone who is willing to openly discuss his feelings.

4. Non-smoker — This was important to me because the smell of smoke conjures up negative memories of my childhood.

5. No "Baby Mama Drama" — Men with young kids typically come with baggage that I knew I was not prepared to deal with, and there was too much risk of being abandoned and hurt.

With much thought and prayer, I willingly started on a path to develop a deep friendship with the man from the church that could lead to marriage. During the time we dated, a phrase was coined... "Court, Pursue, and Woo!"

Court

Courtship is a relationship between a man and a woman in which they seek to determine if it is God's will for them to marry each other.

Pursue

Instead of pursuing "the one," the Bible teaches us to chase after Jesus, who is the One. In Genesis, both Adam and Eve had a relationship with God before they had a relationship with each other. They knew how to love each other because they had experienced God's love for them.

Not only had TMFTC (the man from the church) mastered the art of courtship, he quickly put me on notice that his pursuit game was like no other. You see, being a man of God, he understood a few key things:

- Many of us go through life trying to find "the one" and we focus our efforts on finding that special someone instead of trying to be that someone.
- The best way to pursue a woman is by chasing after her the way Jesus chased after us. Don't give her your leftovers, and don't make her come to you. Jesus met us where we were, and He gave us His all (Romans 3:23). Pursuing us took sacrifice and pursuing "her" will too.
- A good relationship requires a willingness to be authentic. The man must be comfortable in his own skin. He must be someone who receives his masculine identity from Christ, not from the woman he hopes to marry.

Woo

Try to gain the love of a woman, especially with a view to marriage.

TMFTC proclaimed, "I've decided that I only want 'A' and that's YOU!" He presented me with many thoughtful gifts and has been WOOing me ever since. He became a student and learned what I deemed romantic and what I value. Most importantly, when he got to my heart, he WOOed me like a perfectly choreographed dance... gently leading; careful not to drive, push or drag me around; and, full of great twists and twirls.

My biological clock has stopped ticking. God has blessed me with seven amazing godchildren (Julian, Ashley, Briana, Lyric, Connor, Zuri, and Derrin), but my dream of having children will not happen. I will never bear children, never! I am pleased to say that through it all, God has allowed me to become a wife. At the mature age of 50, I married the man from the church on August 18, 2018. You see, during the crossroads of deciding to have an abortion, I realized that I wanted to be a wife more than I wanted to be a mother. God understood, I'm okay.

SOUL REFLECTION:

In life we experience many trials and tribulations. Through it all, we must forgive others and ourselves along the way. God has commanded that we "do not get tired of doing what is good. At just the right time we will reap a harvest of blessing if we don't give up." (Galatians 6:9). I also like the King James Version of this Scripture which says, "And let us not be weary in well doing: for in due season we shall reap, if we faint not."

The Male Man

DERRICK L. FAGGÉTT

"A good man leaves an inheritance [of moral stability and goodness] to his children's children."

—Proverbs 13:22 AMPC

As I've brought back to remembrance many scenes in my life, I'm reminded metaphorically of a poem I once read called "Footprints." Meaning that God was with me in times I felt He wasn't near. In most cases, although I was unknowing, He carried me through most of my battles.

It's hard to understand life in real time. In fact, it's only after you've survived your endeavor and reflect on it that you realize why you had to go and grow through what you went through!

Many thoughts traveled my mind as a young man growing up in Chicago. The most reoccurring thought was, *Where's my father?* Not having my father in my life to explain why he wasn't with me, what he thought of me, who I am, or who I could be hurt me deeply. So, I became angry, confused, lost, and I behaved in a reckless manner. Feeling abandoned, I despised my father and God at times, mostly because I couldn't trace either when I was in need of them. I've often felt as if I had to prove my self-worth to others as well as to myself. In some instances, I still do it today.

As a young man, I moved to Texas to be closer to my father since he was unwilling to come to me. My hope was that since I'd be closer, we could forge a relationship. Well, that didn't happen, and it left me very disappointed. In search of getting my father's attention, I turned to sports and played at a high level throughout high school. I received a scholarship to a major university to play ball, but it still wasn't enough for me or for my father. He never came to see me play! I was so broken, confused, and filled with uncertainty that I declined that scholarship offer not realizing its long-term potential. I've often regretted that decision; that was one of those times I really needed that fatherly advice. So again, I was disappointed by my father's inability to put me on his list of priorities. That caused me to spiral into a deep depression!

Moving back home, I was still trying to find myself. Thankfully, I never acquainted myself with any narcotic substances. However, my drug of choice was sex, since I no longer had the desire to fill that void with sports.

Throughout my journey of recklessness, my behavior not only affected me negatively but it began to affect others, like the countless women I was sexually involved with. I left a trail of damaged relationships with no sense of commitment while fathering four children out of wedlock. I didn't connect the dots—that God kept me hidden from the enemy's plan for destruction—until much later in life. A number of those illicit encounters with various women were unprotected. At times, I couldn't control my urges nor myself. In trying to describe that uncontrollable feeling today, it would seem as if I was battling between two people—the me who wanted the madness to stop and the me who was in search of a sexual high that crept its way into my life at an early age. This may sound familiar to you; it most definitely did to me! It's the same spirit my father, his father, and his father's father allowed to reach my lineage. When fathers are not present in their children's lives, a multitude of dysfunctions can occur in their absence. Those dysfunctions can include rape, sexual perversion, change in sexual orientation, teen pregnancy, sex trafficking and or molestation, and the list continues!

Unfortunately, my story isn't just my own. This issue spans the globe. Many men have similar storylines dealing with the pathology of fatherlessness. As a result of most men not knowing how to correct this issue much less being willing to discuss it, fatherlessness continues to pass from generation to generation untreated.

I was fortunate to have a praying mom who cared and was wise enough to put me before God. My mother was a no nonsense, straightforward, God-fearing woman who held me accountable for my choices. Although my mother did an amazing job raising me and my siblings on her own, I still needed my father's presence. I thank God for my mom; she did the best she could with what she had! Our mothers stepped up when most of our fathers stepped out. They held down the family for many generations, especially in my community. However, our mothers weren't equipped to teach our men how to be men. Hence the reason why in today's culture we have so many feminized men. Not to mention the affect fatherlessness has on our daughters who would then demonstrate the do's and don'ts in selecting a mate.

I've had one maybe two epiphanies in life, but this one was the most defining! It was my forty-first birthday year. I'd experienced a few successes in my life, but most were short-lived. Bankrupt financially, emotionally, physically, and spiritually, I was at rock bottom! Everything that meant anything in my life, including my family, had disintegrated. It was at that point that I recognized clearly that I had become the very person I rarely had a chance to see or get to know... my father! On one of those lonely nights of feeling sorry for myself, I had a disturbing dream. I was standing over my body at my own funeral. My four children were there as well... crying. They couldn't hear me nor see me, but I could hear them as my two oldest daughters began to speak one at a time.

Long story short, the things they had to say weren't pleasing at all. My two younger children were too small to understand what was really going on; however, they would always be reminded of that moment as the last time with their father. I began to weep uncontrollably as my body was being lowered into the ground. I woke up, frantically reaching into the air as tears streamed down my face. Quickly, without question, I got on my knees to pray for forgiveness and a way to rewrite my narrative because I didn't want that ending. Even though it was just a dream, it was clearly a warning. I'd always felt in my spirit God whispering to me, "Neither you nor your children were mistakes! This doesn't have to be your story, Derrick. If you don't like this ending ONLY YOU have the power to change it!"

It was on that day in February 2012, living in a motel, that I forgave my father. Not for him, but for me and my children. It was time to be the better man and father. I rededicated my life to Christ wholeheartedly and formed a covenant declaration with God to no longer accept or allow the proclivity of fatherlessness to run rampant in my legacy going forward. Here's some transparency for you, I thank God for my father's decisions. Why? Because it made me who I am today—a giver! I didn't feel this way during the process of figuring out who or what I was going to be; however, I love my father and always will. You only get one father. He made his choices, now I have to make mine as a man and father!

So, I accepted the challenge to rewrite the newfound chapter of my life. I would not place the blame on what others did or didn't do but instead change what was in my control: me and my decisions. God had a purpose for my pain, but I had to own it first. We all do! So, I created a new normal for myself by making those calls that I'd prolonged to each of my children. If anyone could understand the impact after hearing your father's voice calling to check on you, it would be me since it was what I'd longed for. Now, we have to give what we never received from our earthly fathers but always wanted and that is the love we received from our heavenly Father.

Through seeking wise counsel on corrective behaviors of fatherhood, God continued to surround me with other men that shared my beliefs and visions. I've met so many men who are suffering in the area of being a father because they never had their own fathers. It's a fact that most men who haven't taken the time to build sustainable relationships with their children over time feel that it's too late to do so. In fact, if they mustered up the courage to want to reach out, many wouldn't know where to begin! My recommendation to you is to simply begin and begin simply by being consistent in your actions. Do what you say and be clear with what you mean. In other words, follow through on your commitments. Earn the trust back one step at a time! I've learned that when your intentions are good, the fruits of these actions are always sweeter! It's important to understand that this process isn't about being perfect, but more about being present.

It is my belief that to become this man that I'm speaking of, one must first be willing to admit that he hasn't been that man. We need to rely on one another to get there. Many men have never had the role of a father exemplified correctly so remember this hint: You were once that child who desired what you now have the opportunity to give. It is a gift! This is a key relationship principle for reestablishing dialogue and bridging that gap. Also, keep in mind that it's a marathon not a sprint! You may, in fact, be daddy but you have not been a father! This is the journey to restoration and God's revelation to me on how to foster sustainable relationships with my own children. In addition, you will become that man, father, husband, and the kingdom man you were created to be.

Today, my relationship with my children is a healthier one. I navigate my lifetime goals, decisions, commitments, and priorities around them. They are my legacy. Through prayer and alignment with God's plan, His purpose for me was revealed. It took me a long time to understand why God allowed so much pain and discomfort to enter my life. Had I not experienced the emptiness of fatherlessness, I wouldn't be able to relate to others or have the mental capacity to help change this epidemic. *God doesn't call you just because you are equipped. He, in fact, equips you when you answer the call.* I answered that call!

I'm very meticulous about how I spend my time these days. With whom or on what is of the utmost importance. One of my life's commitments is to live FULL OUT with NO regrets. It's really easy to decide what I focus my attention on. If it's not for the betterment of my family, moving us forward in life, or part of my destiny, I don't do it... period! Another commitment is not getting to the end of my life and wishing I'd said this, done that, or prevented an incident from happening! We only get one shot at this life. One shot at the opportunity to impact our children's lives in a positive way. This thought captures the essence of my existence; yet, it quickened my spirit to move to action. That's why we as a family make it a point to live in the moment by capturing images either by photos or videos. Spontaneity has become a family friend which we've enjoyed when it's time to check off those bucket list items. We do what we want... when we want... as long as we want... with each other!

Since 2012, I've worked extremely hard on myself, my relationship with God, and my willingness to be in tune with His will for my life. He's blessed me immensely with the ability to give life to others through words of wisdom. In my times of prayer, I've asked that when I speak in public or private that He speaks through me, and that He continues to give me a clear vision of His plans for my ordered steps along with a how-to spirit. I remember the day God spoke these words into my spirit, "If you do what I want you to do,

I'll do what you need me to do." I cried like a baby because I knew what He wanted me to do would change lives forever.

SOUL REFLECTION:

The one thing that we all have in common is time. However, no one is privy to its expiration. It's imperative that you decide what you're going to do with the time you have remaining! This fatherless issue is deeply rooted spiritually. It is a trick of the enemy to destroy the foundations of the family order. Satan is very much aware of this demise of The Male Man and we've fallen victims to his plan. But, it isn't too late! It's my belief that God is raising up an army of righteous men of valor who aren't afraid to reclaim their roles as kingdom men. So, Male Men, we have the following decisions to make and the obligation to deliver on God's promises! Fathers and soon to be fathers, a call to action to restore the family dynamic is in full force. If you are a father-less child or you failed in being the father you once desired, YOU can continue this cycle into the next generation or YOU can decide to be an agent of change. Please believe, YOU not making the decision to be the better father has proven to be catastrophic and is in fact... a decision!

The Journey to Freedom Can't Start Without You

SHARON R. CLINTON

*"In their hearts humans plan their course, but
the Lord establishes their steps."*

—Proverbs 16:9 (NIV)

Dear God, it's me, Your daughter. I know you have been waiting and I know this chapter has been almost 30 years in the making, so I ask Your forgiveness for not trusting Your promises enough to leap before, but I remain eternally grateful that as You promised, Your truth would be there to catch and comfort me! Amen!

Has anyone ever asked you for your broken pieces?

I feel like God has been asking for mine for as long as I can remember. Equally, His love escaped my grasp because my view of love was jaded by suffering.

My story is one of growing up in a house that was never truly a home. It was a structure erected in our hearts, built on generations of lies, pain, and deceit. To this day, no one in my family will really acknowledge our true story, but instead meander in the sins of our forefathers and mothers which, until now, has held reign over my voice! Abandoned, sexually violated, emotionally and physically abused—anger and sadness became my drugs of choice. They became all too familiar, and I learned to cope with and more importantly mask them from my everyday life—including in church.

As a young girl, I was an avid reader and escaped the pain by cuddling up in any nearby closet with a book to drown out the destruction happening around me. It might surprise you to know that Judy Blume, a children's author of a book, *Dear God, It's Me Margaret,* was my first introduction to the need for an intimate relationship with God. Though controversial in content, this book provided a realistic view of a teenage girl, who like me, was struggling to fit in with the worlds view of "normal." Like her, I was "growing up" with conflicting views of the world, religion, and relationships, and couldn't help but notice the contradictions between what I heard at church and the pain I was experiencing in my home life.

As an adult looking back at my very real human experience with a heavenly perspective, I can't rule out that suffering seems to be both a calling and a curse, with us as "named partners with Christ" sharing in His suffering (1 Peter 4:13), detailed best in Bruce and Stan's: *God Is In the Tough Stuff.* While this tool travels with me daily now, it didn't show up in time to prevent my suffering from turning my living into mere survival.

Back then, anger hid behind the smile of expectation and false joy. Expectation to be the best, expectation to be loved, expectation of escape and a longing for this great joy I was supposed to consider during trials. Like Margaret, my expectations of the very power of God was in question, and needing true relationship wasn't even processed, as I prayed to God to reveal Himself to me in tangible ways.

How would you describe your current relationship with Christ?
What are you currently suffering from that no one knows about?

You might even still question God's allowance for suffering. It was hard for me too! I didn't understand the need to question the lies, reminding myself of His promises so that grace could enter in. I must tell you, for me it was the only way to the other side of through.

So, where do you begin? Well, it won't be through dressing it up or behaving as if the pain isn't present. You don't have to have it all together. **If you were my friend,** I would tell you it's time to let your heart finally break, have that ugly cry, then sit in your truth. Figure out your triggers— the lies that cause you to tailspin out of control; concentrate on them. Hold them captive the way they have been holding you in bondage. Then, individually and specifically, begin rooting them out—deadening every lie you've ever known. **It is only then that the truth becomes believable.**

Jada Edwards advises in *The Captive Mind* that "We are at war."

*"For though we walk in the flesh, we are not
waging war according to the flesh."*

—2 Corinthians 10:3

I recognized my complacency—waging war against the world with almost none of my beliefs about it backed up with God's truth. So, no more acting like nothing was wrong. I wanted more than the fleeting satisfaction of my anger, anxiety, and depression leaving for a few days or months because of self-soothing. I needed real change. **Do you?**

What thoughts run recklessly through your mind daily? How do they shape what you believe about yourself? What you believe about God?

So, let's start unpacking. I will go first.

*"Even if my father and mother abandon me,
the Lord will take care of me."*

—Psalm 27:10

You want to know what I believed about God? **Almost nothing!** I questioned everything as a child. In a follow up novel, *Are You There God? It's Me, Margaret*, Judy Blume seemed to capture my incessant need for answers as trials seemed to be stitched into my everyday clouds.

Why doesn't my mother love me?
Why would God allow this?
Where is God when pain's hand strikes?
Doesn't He love me?

With constant physical and emotional abuse and the scarcity of truth and love, I began to accept this as life's normal. Never exposing my pain but creating imaginary worlds in my journals where girls who looked like me had cookies on the counter waiting when they arrived home from school, instead of curse words that would destroy my identity for almost 20 years. Terms like black, blacky (as the darkest child in the house), and even a name to describe a female dog would become common as I sank further and further into my pain. So, who would cry for the little black girl?! Not even me! In fact, I stopped crying at all for a time.

Even my relationships with my siblings suffered, as we all began to unknowingly take pain's impact out on each other. Pains no children should ever see or experience, creating scars that would last us all what still feels like a lifetime. My oldest brother, Jeff, would die trying to numb these pains. See, I no longer remember how many times he was put out of the house, starting at age 12, but I still painfully remember my older sister feeding him through the windows of our home. The very same windows I would escape abuse through.

Even with gang violence at an all-time high, police raids, and death at my doorstep, I still somehow managed to walk myself around the corner, every Sunday, searching for this illusive love that seemed to be on everyone's faces except mine. When I couldn't find it, I turned to the world, becoming pregnant at age 17 with my first son. With no more instruction or truth of God's promises than I had before his birth, I became a mother. What was I to do now? My escape plan, derailed. College acceptance letters, shredded! Not only did I now have someone else to plan for, I still hadn't figured a way out for myself! I still had so many more questions. And with each question mark, my identity in Christ moved further and further away.

See, it wouldn't be long before suffering returned. I can still hear the sirens of the police cars and the ambulance that rushed to my aid when my sons' father, who had been stalking me, attempted to take my life. These recollections are but a glimpse into the pain I've carried around with an undesirable stench of pride and bitterness that has done nothing but wreak havoc in my life. It has impacted my decisions, derailed divine appointments, and introduced me to death. You would think that would have been the point where I threw my hands up and waved the proverbial white flag, but no! The more life spiraled, the more I felt I needed to take control of it versus giving it over to the one who created it.

Have you ever believed you weren't good enough?
Have you told yourself that things would never change?

All lies! See, I believed that God made no promises of a good life, but I didn't read further to learn of joy and peace that was only available in His presence. His peace would help me navigate the hard times and He would help me carry the load.

"These things I have spoken to you, so that in Me you may have peace. In the world you have tribulation, but take courage; I have overcome the world."—John 16:33

When we don't deal with our pain, anger takes over. I had to acknowledge my anger towards God. Though I cringe at the thought of that now, asking Him to both restore my belief in Him and His will for my life opened my heart to love again. Not love based on what I could do but handing over my heart so that God could do what I could not!

Trying to figure it out on my own had simply not been working. I am not sure of your path, but I had to leave the place that was rooted in war—my childhood town—so that I could find peace. So, I packed up and moved from California to Texas. There were no fireworks, but for the first time in almost 30 years, I slept through the entire night. I knew then that taking that one step towards healing was about to change my life.

Not all that long ago, I found true answers. In my quest for the truth of who I was to God, I asked to be discipled. During that time, I was introduced to Larry Crabb's book, *Inside Out*. If you decide to use this tool, and **I recommend that you do, be ready!** This book provided retrospective and introspective ideas surrounding not only who I was, but it challenged the very nature of who I thought God could be. It was refreshing and crippling at the same time.

It taught me that breaking down didn't mean that I would fall apart! It showed me that not only did I fear facing Christ, but I feared seeing myself and all my flaws. I was too afraid to cry, too afraid to feel, too afraid to focus on the reality of my pain. Pain had become a second skin and in a crazy way, I was comforted by it. I was learning something new that was flat out scary. I had already proved to not be a "Perfect Christian!" But I found out I am so glad I am not! My brokenness was all He was looking for. No perfection, only progress.

> "For I consider that the sufferings of this present time are not worth comparing with the glory that is going to be revealed to us."
>
> —Romans 8:18

What is in you is going to come out of you. You don't need to break to give Him your brokenness. When I fell from exhaustion, He caught me. He knew I was angry, even at Him, but He still allowed me in. He knew I was fearful, but He still held me. He knew all my sins and He still forgave me. He sent mercy and grace to sit beside me in the night in discipleship and when morning came—new mercies. I had not physically died, but I realized I had died to myself and the brokenness was met by His strength. What's more, I was right where He wanted me to be. Surrendered. Surrendered to His will, whose sovereignty was better than any scheme or plan that I could think of to escape. He had taken the wounds of a little girl's heart and used them to help create change in the hearts of other women. For once love seemed real, attainable, even actionable! Who could have known? HIM! He had been waiting all along for me to act, for me to take the first step so that I could begin again and His glory could win.

I've only scratched the surface in sharing and **change is still happening for me**. The calming qualities of God's truth have finally given way to the confidence that God has everything under control!

I no longer pick up a pen attempting to control all the outcomes. I can finally sit in His presence, feeling no judgment and allowing Him to write my song. My voice has been freed to sing the musical score that could only be crafted by a sovereign and great composer. A feeling of boldness pumped into my lower register producing bold notes of gratitude and a praise that only freedom and love can provide. Breathe it in! It's available for you, too! So, I have one last question.

Will you now take one, or maybe one more, step towards God today?

You can no longer turn left when you know what's right. It's time to do the work!

SOUL REFLECTION:

Dear God, it's me, Sharon! Lord, let me never forget that trials have purpose and don't serve to trash my emotions or weigh down my spirit. Let me never forget that your grace is not common but unmerited favor! Let me never forget that this journey is not just about a change of environment, but a heart overhaul! Help me daily to put to death my desires so I only desire your will! Amen.

The lies we tell ourselves can be paralyzing, and mine cut deep! Believing those lies caused me to push others away and often caused me to hurt even more! What I know now is that we don't often see the world as it is, we see it as we are, and I have a responsibility in this thing. I must stay connected and invested. That means connected in prayer and His Word and invested in things that edify my spirit, my frame of mind, and my peace! Please make no mistake about it, this is a lifelong journey. He will always be there waiting for you to make a move so that He moves mountains in your life! And like me, I hope you find contentment in knowing that every trial is an opportunity for you learn, and grow closer to Him and stronger in your purpose! God has your back! He is my greatest love and He is your biggest fan! **You ask, "Do you still have insecurities?" Well, sure.** But now I am equipped with the truth! I know who I am, I am His!

"The instruction of the Lord is perfect, renewing one's life; the testimony of the Lord is trustworthy, making the inexperienced wise."

—Psalm 19:7

Continued blessings on the journey.

Liv On

JOLANDA K. HARRIS

"For I know the plans I have for you," declares the Lord, "plans to prosper you and not to harm you, plans to give you hope and a future."

—Jeremiah 29:11 (NIV)

No one is an accident. We are created purposely by and for God. Our purpose is to glorify His kingdom while here on Earth. But are we living our earthly purpose?

Over the past 37 years, I have often asked myself: What is my purpose?

I've always admired those who are living in their purpose. How awesome is that! They get to wake up every morning and just *know* what they are supposed to do and where to go; they just live life without reserve each day. There are people who have been living their purpose since the beginning of their life, as if from the moment they could walk, and there are others who will have the privilege of finding themselves when they are teenagers. If not in their teens, then maybe people will suddenly get what they are here for in their 20s, 30s, or discover it in their 50s.

My purpose came to me in what you may consider the most unexpected of ways. In December 2017, I was diagnosed with cancer. Immediately after I received my diagnosis, my next action was to divorce my husband. You may be thinking, "Whaaaat?" and "What did he have to do with you getting cancer?" I know, but I can explain. Let me rewind a bit and take you back to the beginning, before I was diagnosed, before I had to worry about tomorrow, back when I was younger and when my mind could only focus on one thing at a time...

I met my husband, Andre, in 1979 on a bus trip to Opryland Amusement Park. It was your typical, romantic "boy meets girl" that ignited an eight-year relationship. As the relationship grew, Andre joined the armed forces and moved to Florida, and I was preparing to attend college. Determined to still see each other, the long distance put a strain on our relationship. We would later go our separate ways. For Andre, he married and had a family. I, on the other hand, lovingly lived the independent, single life filled with family, friends, and achieving my career ambitions.

In 2008, Andre's wife passed from cancer. It wasn't until 2011 that he and I reconnected and the old flame that started on a trip to Opryland rekindled. We married in 2012. We took another stab at maintaining a long-distance relationship, which turned out to be successful. We were able to manage until January 2014 when I moved from Dallas, Texas, to where he was in Huntsville, Alabama. Marriage was as close to perfect as it could be, until December 2017 when the fairytale came to a screeching halt. I was diagnosed with breast cancer. Instead of laughing and opening Christmas gifts, Andre and I were telling the kids and family what was ahead of us and my treatment plan.

Knowing that Andre lost his first wife to cancer and being told that I had cancer instilled a deep fear in me that he could possibly lose me too. I did not want my husband to relive that nightmare. While looking up my attorney's number to make an appointment, I called my sister and told her my plans. She told me that God gave me a man who was equipped to handle my situation and travel the journey with me. Little did I know my cancer would lead me closer to my purpose down the road.

Now let's fast forward. It was 2:46 a.m., and I was lying in bed asking myself, *How did I get here? How did I get here, stricken with this thing called cancer that was totally unraveling the so-called normal life of myself and my family?* I would lie in bed listening to my husband snore in the middle of the night, thinking, *How am I going to get cancer and hold this family together?*

In the beginning of my journey, those thoughts would be at the forefront of my mind for many sleepless nights. Until I decided enough was enough. Instead I thought, *This is cancer and worrying is not a cure. If I want to beat this, I've got to fight it. I'm going to get it before it gets me.* It was then that I came to the conclusion that I was going to take this journey JoLanda style. I was going to be me and do it my way and on my own terms. And that I did.

Cancer is not a pretty thing. I remember having uncontrollable diarrhea one night. Getting up every five minutes going to the bathroom. There was even one time I thought it was just gas and was trying to make it to the bathroom and I ended up pooping on myself. To me, it was the most degrading of all the things I have experienced in my journey. I recall my husband Andre later looking at me and saying with a straight face, "Baby, you just can't trust the fart." We laughed. My sister was right. My husband was truly equipped to handle this cancer journey.

After that, I decided to have a hair shaving party and invited all my girlfriends over for champagne. After the shave, I donated my hair to Locks for Love. That shaving party was me handling cancer JoLanda style. All on my terms. I did not want to experience seeing 38 inches of hair on the shower floor one morning, so I decided to do me and not wear wigs. I went bald and did me.

During that time, my driver's license expired, and I had to take my photo with no hair. I felt good in my spirit about it. I even got confirmation when I entered the local DMV building and a young lady stopped me and said, "You are rocking that look!"

You can find humor in the oddest places when battling cancer. During one of my treatments, someone on the treatment team would give me steroid shots. The steroid had to be administered slowly and they would ask you how you are feeling as they administered the shot. So, the first time I received the shot, I noticed a reaction but said that I was okay. Then the second time it was administered, by a male nurse, I also told him I was okay. When the nurse left, I told my husband that the steroid made my hoo-ha tingle. His eyes got big and a smile came across his face.

I laughed and said, "Not that way." He could not help but to laugh too. During my next treatment, there was an older woman who had the same steroid administered and she said she had "ants" down there and they were biting. The shameless expression she had in her voice made us all die laughing with her. It turns out my hoo-ha tingling and her "ants" biting are normal reactions to the steroid.

My journey is filled with many days of laughter, pain, and struggle, and I'm still making it through. On my last day of treatment, I made it a party for all of those who gave so tirelessly and selflessly of themselves to my treatment and wellbeing. I gave little tokens of love and gifts to all of my treatment nurses, my doctor, social workers, nurses, lab technicians, and scheduler. I reached a milestone in my journey.

Although I was done with chemo, I still had a ways to go when it came to treatment. Before my double mastectomy, I had to decide whether I wanted to keep my nipples or not. I never realized how important nipples are until forced to make that decision. As I read and researched that your nipples could die if you keep them or decide to re-attach them, Andre took me on a mini trip to get away. While traveling, we discussed the situation and I decided not to keep them due to the risk of cancer reoccurring and not wanting to have another surgical procedure if they die. We left the conversation at that for a while until we were in the Von Maur accessory department. I was trying on a fascinator (I was still bald at the time) and a lady came up to me and asked, "Do you have cancer?" I said, "Yes." Then out of nowhere she told me, "So did I and my nipples died." I didn't know that lady from Adam and I'd never seen her before in my life, but her direct, random comment was something I needed to hear. I hugged her and thanked her for the confirmation I was not aware I was looking for. We chatted then went our separate ways.

After my mastectomy, I underwent 28 days of radiation. I remember so vividly treatments where I could (painlessly) feel the radiation on my breast coming through to my back.

During my five months of continuous chemotherapy, I developed neuropathy in my hands and my feet, which gives me a continuous numbness and a tingly and achy feeling. Cancer has a way of sticking around!

In October, I went to a follow-up visit with my general surgeon. With big plans to celebrate the great news, I asked him, "When will I be cancer free?" To my surprise, he more or less told me, "Never." In his explanation, my surgeon told me that I will always have cancer in my lymph nodes. Taken aback, I thought in awe, *I'll never get rid of this—I'll always have cancer.* Along with, *What the &·$!#% did you just say?* After that news I was left pondering, *What am I supposed to do with this, Lord?*

After completing chemotherapy, a double mastectomy, radiation, and maintenance chemotherapy for a year, my oncologist called and wanted to talk to us. When we went for the appointment, he wanted to put me on a fairly new oral chemotherapy drug for another year, but the side effects were aggressive. I would be the first of his patients to have the traits and characteristics necessary to take the drug. Being the first to try a new drug was daunting, but I told him if I did not take the drug then how would he know if it will help others in the future? I was willing to make that leap for my sake and for his too.

I had been on this journey for almost two years, and it was not until that point that my purpose became clear: I was getting phone calls and texts from friends and family that wanted me to talk with relatives and acquaintances who were diagnosed and going through the cancer journey. I would oblige, and to my surprise, I found myself on a high when talking to others about my experiences. Talking with others about the ups and downs of treatment, calming their fears, getting support, and forming new bonds inspired me. I developed a yearning deep inside to do more, to help someone who is in the battle and needs a lil' pep.

My family continuously stayed by my side through every step of my journey, especially my well-equipped husband. My brother and sister-in-law would drive from North Carolina to Alabama to be with me for my weekly chemotherapy treatments. My sister left her home in Florida to stay during the 12-week period and my parents were there every time.

Because I was so blessed throughout my journey, I wished to be a blessing to a cancer patient at the Institute for Christmas. So, I asked my family if we could not exchange gifts that season, but instead, I wanted them to join me in supporting a cancer patient that was having some financial difficulty. They agreed to help, and I called the Institute and asked for a family in need of additional support. The social worker told me that all of the families had been taken care of.

Taken aback, I questioned, surely there was one family that was left? She told me that she would look into it. I called back every day, until thankfully, there was one family. We were provided a Christmas list from the family. Then, I asked the social worker if she would get permission from the family to connect with them because we wanted to go beyond the list. The family agreed. On Christmas Eve, we provided the ultimate Christmas dinner, toys, and spiritual blessings to that family. And from showing them love through their difficult time in treatment, we are now forever bonded. The granddaughter calls us Nana Jo and Papa Andre. The grandmother said that she feels good to know that if anything happens to her, her granddaughter will have us. That urged me to devote time to the Institute. And with that, everything came together. My supporting husband and his earlier cancer journey with his first wife and my confidence throughout my experiences with cancer all led up to the discovery of my purpose.

God finally revealed my new purpose. But, in order to do that He had to: 1.) Get my attention, 2.) Teach me that cancer is not the end of my story, and 3.) Show others how to successfully live with cancer and other major illnesses.

God is blessing me to be able to survive and live on with cancer in my body to let those out there know that there are people who win the battle of cancer and people who continuously fight on the battlefield of cancer. Regardless of where you are on the spectrum, just know that the battle is what you make it.

Our purpose is not in the adventure, not in the ambition, not in the accolades or the aspirations, it's in the journey.

There are multitudes of us who will always be living with cancer and other major illnesses along with those who are survivors. I'm here to help others through the journey of finding their purpose in life, but most importantly to inspire them to LIVE ON! That's my re-purpose.

SOUL REFLECTION:
The purpose is in the journey.

Love Lifted Me

DRETONA T. MADDOX

*"He pulled me out of a dangerous pit, out of the deadly quicksand.
He set me safely on a rock and made me secure. He taught me
to sing a new song, a song of praise to our God. Many who
see this will take warning and will put their trust in the Lord."*

—Psalm 40:2-3

It was revival week at our home church. The guest evangelist preached a fiery message entitled "Draw the Line." She was very charismatic, and her presentation of the gospel message moved me to tears. As the service came to an end, she began to call individuals to the altar to pray for them. She laid hands on them, whispered something in their ears, and they began to cry aloud in the sanctuary as if they had heard the voice of God. My curiosity grew from their reactions, and the more I watched, the more I felt compelled to get in the long prayer line and ask for her to pray for me. As I got closer to her, I began to weep uncontrollably. I was next in line. I took one step forward. She asked me to lift my hands in surrender to God and she said two words, "Forgive her."

My earliest memory of childhood goes back to the age of two years old. My family—my brother (who is three years my elder) and my mother—lived in a small, modest home in the South Central area of Los Angeles, California. I also have an older sister who is four years my elder, but she did not live with our family. My sister has cerebral palsy, a physical disability that affects movement and posture, and she lived in a facility for disabled children. My sister could not walk or talk. She communicated by making sounds. She also laughed a lot. My family visited my sister once a week, and she would scream and cry every time we left her at the facility. When we would arrive at home after leaving my sister behind, my mother would go to her room and shut the door behind her, leaving me and my brother with the impossible task of processing our emotions about what just happened. Although I was very young, I was clear about the pain that my family experienced as a result of leaving my sister in that facility.

I have memories of my mother going to work dressed in a white dress, white nylons, white shoes, and a white nursing cap. Between the age of two and three, I didn't know that my mother was a nurse, but I knew that she was happy when she left home. I enjoyed watching her get dressed, but I have no memory of her ever giving me a hug or a kiss or even saying goodbye before she left the house. I just know that she left. And when she returned, she would proceed to her bedroom and shut the door behind her without ever greeting me with a hello. Her room sat at the front of the house on the left side. The curtains in her bedroom were always closed, and no light shined through the window. I believe that she worked the night shift. I cannot recall who babysat me when she was at work, but I know my brother was my primary caretaker. What seemed like every day, he cooked for me sticky white rice with sugar and ketchup. He also prepared mayonnaise sandwiches for me before he left for school on his bike.

I also have memories of my mother partying—wearing Vidal Sassoon jeans, a polyester long sleeve shirt, and thigh-high camel colored boots. She had such a beautiful Coca-Cola bottle body shape; she was small in the waste and thick in the hips. As we would walk up to the stairs to the apartment where the house party was being held, the music would be blasting so loud that it could be heard from the curb. My heart would pound with excitement as my little legs would struggle up the stairs as I carried my pillow and blanket. The host of the party would welcome my mother as she approached the apartment door. The living room area was lit with red lights, and she would start dancing as soon as she passed the entryway of the smoke-filled room. My brother and I had to stay in one of the bedrooms. But, while we were supposed to be asleep, we could not help but crack the bedroom door and glare at her as she would dance the night away to the tune of "Brick House" by the Commodores. I loved seeing her dance. She was the life of the party.

Other memories that invade my mind regularly are not as pleasant as the memories of her dressing up in her white uniform and going to house parties. My mother was involved in an unhealthy relationship, and it caused a lot of fear and uncertainty in our home. My mother and her partner would physically fight, and some fights would lead to one or both of them requiring hospitalization. For my brother and I, our bedroom became our safe haven from the violence, and the bed became our shield. When the arguing would start, we would run into our bedroom, hide under the bed, and cover our ears until the noise would stop. However, nothing could prevent us from hearing the violent thrusts against the walls.

Sadness and anger with a ray of sunshine was the norm in our home. Some days were filled with laughter, but most days, there was an overwhelming presence of darkness looming. Then one day, my 26-year-old mother succumbed to the tormenting pain of living and ended her life on Earth. I was four years old.

As I went through pre-adolescence, I began to yearn for my mother intensely. I couldn't sleep at night, and I felt like I couldn't bear the thought of not having a mother. Although my maternal grandmother had become the legal guardian of my siblings and I after my mother's death, I felt like nothing and nobody could ever fill the hole in my heart and the emptiness that I held onto deep down within my soul. I identified with the darkness that once loomed over my home and invited it to stay with me. It was familiar. However, the comfort of knowing that I could rely on depression to keep me company did not prevent rage from cultivating inside of me. Prolonged and complicated grief, coupled with an intense longing for my mother, had manifested itself into contempt. I hated her.

I hated my mother for leaving me. I hated her for every sleepless night. I hated her for all the years that I needed a confidant, a nurturer, an advocate. I hated her for missing every Mother's Day celebration. I grew up in the Baptist church, and every year on Mother's Day, the Mother's Board of the church would adorn me with a white carnation flower which is used to honor a mother who is dead. I hated her not being there to pick me up when I fell down or to hug me when I was hurt. I hated her for not being there for my first crush and my first break-up. I hated her because when I was 15 years old, I got pregnant, and because I was homeless and had to rely on strangers to give me shelter, I aborted my child. I hated her for missing my high school graduation and my wedding day. I hated her for not being there for the birth of my children and for my children not having a maternal grandmother. I hated her because I needed her.

For many years as an adult, I struggled with trying to make sense of my mother's death by suicide. I tried to find peace with all of the unanswerable questions that lingered in my mind. There were moments that I wanted to replay fond memories or share stories of my childhood, but that could not be done without nostalgia. It became agonizing to allow my mind to connect with thoughts of her. To cope with the intense pain that I felt almost daily, "Her death and her choice" became my mantra. I believed and accepted that my mother's legacy was pain and sorrow. But God.

"Come to me, all who are tired from carrying heavy loads, and I will give you rest. Place my yoke over your shoulders, and learn from me, because I am gentle and humble. Then you will find rest for yourselves because my yoke is easy, and my burden is light."

—Matthew 11:28-30

After receiving prayer from the evangelist during our church revival service, I pondered over the words that the evangelist had spoken to me, "Forgive her." I wrestled with the notion that the Lord had revealed to the evangelist that I hated my mother. Thoughts like, *She don't know me! She doesn't know what I have been through in my life! Nobody knows what I feel about my mother, so there is no way she could be talking about my feelings towards my mother!* flooded my brain. The more I fought, the more I cried as God confirmed in my spirit that it was time to repent from my sin of hatred. I had held on to it long enough. And although I had not spoken those words to anyone, God knew, and He assured me that He was there to forgive me as I forgave my mother.

Forgiving my mother was one of the hardest things I had ever done. I asked God, "How am I supposed to forgive a person who is dead?" I couldn't call on the phone to discuss the devastation that she had left behind. I couldn't ask her, "Why didn't you love me enough to live?" I felt what God was requiring of me to do was impossible. As I laid on the floor crying, praying, and begging for guidance, God began to minister to my spirit, and He impressed upon me that I had believed a false report. My mother did not leave me a legacy of pain and sorrow; instead, I was a child of God through faith in Christ Jesus, which made me an heir of God and a co-heir with Christ. The fact is, my mother suffered from depression—a mental health disorder that negatively alters the way you feel, think, and behave. My mother believed that death was her only solution for living without pain. Her death was not about me. Her death was about her. The more I prayed, the more I understood that my mother was sick and needed help; help that I would have never been able to give. With that revelation, I no longer felt bound by grief and sadness. I felt that God had a purpose for my pain. I then prayed and denounced all the hatred that I had within my heart for my mother. I asked God to forgive me as I forgave her, and I vowed to honor her name.

I don't pretend to know all of the reasons why my mother chose to take her own life. I still sometimes struggle with the concept of her altering the plan of her life by committing suicide. Some days it's hard to wrap my mind around the idea of choice as it relates to death and some days I feel out of sync. I also still have conversations with God about the purpose of it all. However, I no longer live in the shadow of her death. I am no longer tormented with the pain of grief and loss. God loves me so much that He used an evangelist during a revival service to expose my secret sin. He used her to speak two simple words, "Forgive her."

SOUL REFLECTION:

A death by suicide will always be considered nothing short of a tragic loss. It is a loss that is not easily explained or understood. For those suffering from depression, suicide may feel like the only way to relieve the unendurable pain of living, but for those left behind, the grief of a suicidal loss can be so devastating and life-altering that it feels like you will never be able to put the broken pieces of your life back together again. Your pain from the loss can become a breeding ground for feelings of anger, resentment, and even hatred. But God.

I am in awe of His love for mankind. The way He demonstrates His love for us is far beyond comprehension. You see, it was never my intention to hide my sin of hatred from God. I was simply ignorant of the depths of my transgression, but God knows His creation better than we know ourselves. And He loved me so much that He didn't allow me to continue to walk around unaware of the poisonous hatred that was eating at my soul. Forgiveness is a gift, and I am honored to be a recipient.

If you feel depressed and you have thoughts of harming yourself, please #gethelp! And if you know someone that has expressed thoughts of harming themselves, please #gethelp! Suicide is one-hundred percent preventable.

National Suicide Prevention Lifeline:
1-800-273-TALK (8255)

Reinvest Your Favor

CYNTHIA FOX EVERETT

"From the end of the earth I will cry to You, When my heart is overwhelmed; Lead me to the rock that is higher than I."

—Psalm 61:2 (NKJV)

"When we deny our stories, they define us. When we own our stories, we get to write a brave new ending."

—Brené Brown

The sun rose and set on another glorious day. I looked forward to watching three redbirds play and flirt with each other. A demanding bluebird always seemed to interrupt their cue on who would be chased and who would do the chasing. I watched them with a heightened sense of envy. As I watched them from my rear view mirror, the heavy raindrops started to fall wherever Mother Nature deemed necessary. I wondered where my friends took refuge. I started to ponder why my life couldn't be so simple. Was that even a possibility for me? My spirit said yes, but my flesh said no. Could it be possible for Cynthia Morrison Fox Jackson Everett? Only time would tell. In December 2003, I chose to heal, not realizing that it would cause me great misery and pain for a lifetime. I didn't totally count the cost of this journey.

I was first diagnosed at the Fayetteville Veterans Hospital. I was diagnosed with Post-Traumatic Stress Disorder (PTSD), Major Depressive Disorder, Anxiety Disorder, and MST (Military Sexual Trauma). I had served in the U.S. Army for fourteen years. I also served in Desert Shield/ Desert Storm in 1990 for six months. My life hasn't been the same since. After my tour in the war, it felt like someone had reached out and placed a debilitating grip around my throat and squeezed my already fractured heart and soul.

On December 12, 1990, my duty as a soldier would be tested beyond measure. I quickly reminded myself that the way I trained was the way I would live and die. I reminded myself all that day that I hadn't done this before and I had a lot to learn before I was to be exposed to war. We arrived in Saudi Arabia after nine hours of flight from Germany. When we left, we had snow up to our knees. Once we landed, we had to take off most of our clothes; it was about one hundred degrees. We had a hard time adjusting to the weather and adjusting mentally as well. That was one of the longest days of my life. Once we settled in at the port, we were briefed on the rules. We were told not to go anywhere alone. There had been kidnappings and rapes going on. We convoyed into the desert. We ended up stopping because we had a gas leak in one of our tanks. We had to sit on the side of the road and wait for help. Another vehicle stayed with us. It was growing dark and colder. Another convoy came along and rescued us.

By then, we were extra scared, extra tired, and extra hungry, but extra glad because we were rescued. We drove for a while and stopped again. We were thinking, "What now?" I looked to the left and saw someone with our forklift. We didn't give anyone permission. We all got out of our trucks to see what was going on over the dust. A five-ton truck had overturned because of a sudden sandstorm. They were in a ditch. We were trying to see and to assist if need be. There were two soldiers in the truck and one of them was unresponsive. A command decision was made on who they would save. The female soldier was responsive, so they chose her. Her legs were crushed. They flew her back to Germany. The driver was still unresponsive. We stood there with looks that said, "I'm a soldier but I'm also human." All we could do was stare, feeling helpless and hopeless. Because we were soldiers, our tears were invisible. We were all one, again. We all stood watching and paralyzed. Our frozen faces were stuck on the last emotions. We all had the same look. We aren't supposed to leave a soldier behind! How could we fix this? The only thing we could do was pray together again. Our invisible tears left a streak on our dusty, fuel exhausted, heavily smoked skins. They finally got him out of the overturned truck. He was limp, bloody, and looking like a rag doll, but still a soldier. He paid the ultimate price—his life. We learned later that he was twenty-four, just married, and just had a baby. It felt like someone had stabbed us in our chests and twisted the knife.

When the dust settled, we all returned to our trucks with our chilled tears stuck to our faces. We were all silently choking from the pains in our chest. All we wanted was the pain to stop so we could close our eyes and wait for someone to tell us we were dreaming. No, it was officially a nightmare. We wore our guilt like a winter coat laced with needles next to our skin and the buttons were made of scales. It took me over thirty years to forgive myself; but, only after much therapy, medication, and tears. The tears once again sealed it. Sometimes I feel like I abandoned the deceased soldiers that filled the bottom of the plane and the roaming souls that we left in the desert. They were draped in honor with the colors of the flag as their crown and a badge over their hearts. Those colors will never fade. The psychological scars from war never leave you. We learn to cope as best we know how through therapy, groups, and medication. Some have shame and some have guilt left over. It's like you skip a heartbeat then you get back on track. That one heartbeat is held in high regard for the one(s) we left behind.

Having PTSD, depression, and anxiety is like walking around with a boulder hanging around my neck while wrapped in barb wire, never to be shaken loose. I walk around with my own private war going on in my head. Sometimes it gets worse, sometimes it gets better. I dare not go into my own mind alone. I could get lost again and again. I've been in some sort of therapy since 2003. I had to learn to forgive myself for the soldiers we left behind; I still have my days. What I do know is I'm here. And as long as I'm here, why not use what I know and what I have learned?

The Yellow in My Rainbow

My journey back to wellness started in December 2003. I first had to acknowledge that I had a problem and that I wasn't that crazy person my family labeled me to be. I never figured out how I was supposed to "get over it." After a while, I was ready to heal. I admitted to myself that no matter what was broken, I needed it to be fixed. Since I am a Veteran, I made an appointment at the closest Veterans Hospital. It took a little while to get an appointment, but I held on. In the meantime, I prayed for healing and direction. I knew that I had to heal naturally and spiritually as well. On the day of the appointment, I went alone; I was doing it for me first.

I saw a psychiatrist. She was a very nice older woman. We talked for a while and I grew to trust her. Remember that you don't normally share with people that you don't trust. I felt safe on our visits. We discussed the problem, goals, medication, and the best way to get my desired results. She included me in everything we discussed. I always had the final say. This is very important no matter who you see. If possible, see the same person for as long as you can. That establishes consistency. As my life changed, I changed. I didn't have a strong support system in place at the time. My church is my strength. When I feel like I have no one I can count on, my relationship with my church will be there. It is what I call a nonjudgmental place; a safe place to heal. This is also very important in your healing process.

Throughout the years, I've had to change my medications. It's very important to know what you are taking and the side effects. I have some liver damage from a particular medication I take. Depending on your medication, you have to do lab work. Mine is every three months. I became addicted to pain pills. I checked myself into detox and rehab. Again, my meds were adjusted. It's very important to have a balance in your life. Your physical fitness is very important.

Stress is a big factor also. My mind and body let me know when I'm out of sync. I used NA/AA and different therapies as a tool to get back on my feet. I have been in a mental hospital three times and to detox numerous times.

One of the hardest things I've had to do is live unfiltered, clean, and sober. I had been taking four different types of opioids, and medicine for sleep, depression, anxiety, and a few more pills. In total, I was taking about fourteen pills. I took pills to wake up and I took medication to go to sleep. I had been taking them for two and a half years. I told myself that failure isn't an option! I was afraid to be alone. I learned to be strong for my children and grandchildren, but mainly for me! To thine own self be true. Learn your support agencies around you. All these tools will help you get to a place of healing. Most importantly, you must believe in your purpose one more time than you believe in your pain. Remember you are priceless.

SOUL REFLECTION:

Choose every day to forgive yourself and to fall in love with yourself. You are human, not perfect. Most of all, you are worthy of real love.

The Road Trip to Purpose

DAMITA JO CROSBY

*"But as for you, turn you, and take your journey into
the wilderness by the way of the Red Sea."*

—Deuteronomy 1:40 (KJV)

To have and to hold, until death do us part is what I said before God and my family. I truly believed it in my heart. Being the daughter of a single mom, I never wanted to go through what I saw my mother endure. Well, seventeen years later, I found myself filing for divorce with six children! I wasn't completely surprised, but I was still devastated.

Have you ever had to hide all of your depression and anxiety because you were the picture of hope others looked to? Have you ever had to hide from your closest friends and family that the life you have been living is a lie? Well, I'm here to tell you that you are not alone.

How do you know it is really over? Have you done everything possible to save that which you said you would give your life to? There were so many questions I asked myself every day. I felt as though everyone had turned their back on me, especially God. I was truly in the wilderness.

Guess what? Then I decided that I could no longer live in the same city or state with him. Was I crazy? Had I completely stopped hearing from God? I packed up six children and moved to Texas. My road trip to purpose. 1,800 miles in 27 hours... no stopping, just get out. Running for my life. Not my physical life, but my spiritual life. I had hatred and unforgiveness in my heart. I was hurting from a pain I thought would never dissipate. I had a wound that I believed could never be healed. I was blinded by my situation and I couldn't see the rainbow that hovered above me.

Believing God allowed my life as I knew it to end. I was angry, but I also believed He had to have something better for me. But what would it be? And when would He share with me what it was? Days and nights of crying for months yet there was no answer. Waking up in the middle of the night screaming brought no answers. Within three months, my teenage boys were acting out, and still no answer. A daughter placed in my care by the Child Protective Service in California was being called back to California to live with her sister, and still no answer. Now I'd lost a husband and a child. What more could I bear?

People said it was time for me to date. Date? Seriously, I am a woman of God, devoted to my children and church. I really didn't have time for that. I was left again asking God, "Where are you?" I was depressed, I had gained weight, and I barely knew my way around my newfound home. But, I did long for companionship. I wanted to hear the voice of someone who would show some compassion. Of course, I didn't let anyone at church know how I felt. The minute people got too close, I pulled back.

I will encourage you by telling you that I never stopped praying every day—morning, noon, and night. Somedays between my tears all day! And in between the tears, God began to reveal "small" things. How I needed to care for myself. How I needed to fast for direction, not for healing and not for the pain to go away. God told me to get up and get out beyond what had become familiar. He spoke through Scripture. One Scripture in particular, which is now my motto was, "I will bless the Lord at all times: his praise shall continually be in my mouth" (Psalm 34:1). I came to understand that I couldn't base my praise on if I was having a good day. I couldn't just praise Him if my sons decided to act right in school. I couldn't just praise Him when all the bills got paid on time. What I know from the good days and the bad days is that praise is non-negotiable! I decided that I would praise Him no matter what!

When I began to really see God in everything—the tears, my shortcomings, my pain, my joy, my laughter—I gained greater focus. I could understand the Scriptures better. In Psalms where it says, "Thou shalt not be afraid of the terror by night, nor the arrow that flieth by day;" it was clear to me that night was always when the sun goes down.

When I packed up my children and we began our road trip from California to Texas it was 7:00 a.m. Although it was a full 12-14 hours before the sun set, it eventually did. Darkness fell upon the highway, my children went to sleep, and tears rolled down my cheeks. Phone calls came from friends and family telling me to get off the highway, get a motel room for the night, get some rest. But, I couldn't. Something wouldn't allow me to give in to the "night."

Just like I couldn't give in to that night, I couldn't give in to the many nights to come. Many sunny days were dark. On my darkest day, God continued to reveal Himself. Scripture after Scripture came to my lips without reaching for my Bible. God was reminding me that I belonged to Him first. Before I decided to marry a man that I thought was "the one," God showed me that His grace and mercy had been manifested in my life. I had reached a new understanding with God that I would praise him at "night." My night praise became my war cry and my victory shout.

Victory

Just like that, one day I woke up and there were no more tears, only peace. I reached for the Word of God and the Scripture before me said, "Peace I leave with you, my peace I give unto you: not as the world giveth, give I unto you. Let not your heart be troubled, neither let it be afraid" (John 14:27). Well, thank you God. I remember saying, "It's about time!" LOL.

It was a new day; a new dawn of being who God created me to be. Well, not really. I was learning. Well, no, not that either. I was now in a place where I could be taught. I could be molded. I could be made. I could be pruned. Many people go through the pruning process at the darkest hour. Mine came at victory. You may be thinking, why at victory? Why not when you were at your darkest time? Well, God knows me and He knows you. For me, when it was dark, I was too fearful. I was already in pain, so I couldn't take the pruning. I was living in unforgiveness so I couldn't be molded. God had to wait until I truly understood that my road trip through the night was to bring me to victory.

What did victory mean for me? The same thing it means now. I have a purpose. A God ordained plan for my life. A plan that He shall complete until the day of His return. The road trip and every trial that came with it, every bump in the highway, every stop, the glare of everyone else's light shining in my face was to get me to a place where God could talk to me and I would listen. Victory is seeing God in my purpose. Seeing God in every detail is victory.

Don't get me wrong, the road trip that began in 2006 has not ended. There are days that I feel the pain of my children longing for a father who wasn't present. The pain a mother carries for her children when their father remarries shortly after the divorce and assumes the position of father to "the other woman's" child in the home. It is a burden to bear but it has gotten lighter over the years as my children have grown into adulthood. Let me not shortchange God. He allowed me to date and remarry. My husband is a man He designed for me and the children.

The road trip continues to have bumps in the road, for warning, not for harm. There are pit stops to refuel, not to get stuck in a pit. Every day on this road trip is not easy. Every day is a day of prayer. Prayer has been vital to my victory. Remember it was between the tears and prayer that God revealed Himself. Communication with God is an extraordinary gift. He sits waiting just to have a conversation with us. We just need to remember that a conversation is two-way communication. I had to remind myself of that early on in the road trip. Through all my crying and unforgiveness, often I didn't give God a chance to respond to my prayer. Well, really at that point, I didn't want to listen. Victory is in listening. Victory is in receiving correction and redirection from God. Don't be like me with my map of the road, not wanting to detour from dislike, malice, hurt, and pain. These are the very things that made night fall. Remember to think on the things that God directs us to in His Word. Think about past victories, remembering if He did it before He can do it again.

Our God is master and commander of the universe. If He decrees a stop sign, it is for your good. If He decrees a roadblock, it is for your good. If He decrees a bump in the road, hold on. He is sovereign, all mighty, and all powerful. Wow... there was a day when I wouldn't have shared that with you. I recall almost hanging up on my sister as she would assure me that God was listening and directing my life. *Whatever*, I thought, *sure He is.*

He sure is! God is continuing to map out my road trip, if I continue to read the map. Reading and meditating on His Word along with prayer daily is the best map any of us can have. I advise you that whatever state you're in, don't give up. Keep driving. Sometimes the destination won't look the way you think it should look. The people may not be what you expect. The opportunities people tell you about may not suit you. God has THE opportunity of your life. It is victory through the storm. It is victory along your journey. It is the purpose you were born for.

Let me tell you, on my road trip from California ("the land of milk and honey") to Texas, I spoke to many terrains. When we drove through the deserts of Palm Springs and

Arizona, the endless sand and mountains were dry places. I looked out and said, "I know how you feel. My joy is gone, and I am dry." On my way to victory, I drove through cities and states that had no appeal. And I could say, "I know how you feel. I don't appeal to anyone either." Desert storms are an awesome sight to see, but hard to drive through. And I could say, "Storm, you have me hanging on for my life." At the Texas border, I thought, *I'm here.* But it was another 10 hours before I would reach my new home. While driving I thought, *Why would you let me reach the tip and not feel welcome?* Thinking back on my self-talk and my somewhat talk with God on the journey, I am saddened by how little faith I had. Writing this for you to read, I feel somewhat ashamed that I know God and I knew then what God could do, but I was consumed by bends in the road.

SOUL REFLECTION:

If you are in a bend in the road, keep turning. God will lead you to the path that your purpose is on! "For the Son of Man is as a man taking a far journey, who left his house, and gave authority to his servants, and to every man his work, and commanded the porter to watch" (Mark 13:34, KJV). Jesus left the safety of His Father in Heaven to take a journey; to encounter as a man, in flesh, the things that we encounter. His journey led Him to the ultimate sacrifice. And while sacrificing His life, He asked for our forgiveness. My greatest joy now comes from knowing I had to take a road trip to forgive, so that I could step into purpose.

Trials, Trauma, Tragedy, and Triumph!

JANIS BARNES

"I have told you these things, so that in me you may have peace. In this world you will have trouble. But take heart! I have overcome the world."

—John 16:33 (NIV)

Rape, abortion, and breast cancer. Any of these things could cause depression, fear, self-pity, or death. Yet, I am a survivor through the strength of Jesus!

Rape

It was a school day. I was about ten years old. It was in the fall because in Baltimore when the school year first starts the mornings are chilly and you need a sweater or a light jacket. I stopped at the corner store on Chelsea. I bought some Now and Laters and other candy before heading to school. I don't know if he was in the store. I just remember that while I was walking from the store, he approached me saying, "There are some people who want to beat you up, or in Baltimore terms bank you!"

He said, "Come with me. I will hide you from them." I never saw anyone, but I kept running with him. He looked like he was about 18-20 years old. Then, he stopped and said, "Let's hide here." It was under a porch. Once we got under the porch, I realized I was in trouble! He said, "Take your pants and underwear off." I began to think quick and tried to talk him out of it.

He yanked my pants and underwear down. I felt pain and then my bowels moved. Blood and bowels were everywhere; the smell was horrible. I don't remember how I got to school but I did. I made it to the classroom. I was late for school. When I got into the classroom, my teacher came over and rushed me to the restroom. I must have been a mess! I broke down and cried trying to tell her what happened.

I remember my mother coming to the school and riding with me in an ambulance. My father had died when I was six years old. My mother transferred me to another school. I never went to school alone after that day until the seventh grade. Somehow, the kids in other schools outside of the area that we lived in found out and asked me, "Did you get raped?" Embarrassed and ashamed, not realizing that it wasn't my fault, I would say, "No!" I didn't need to be ashamed. I didn't need to hide.

I had given my life to Christ at a young age, and I prayed all the time. Yet, whenever anyone asked me, "Did you get raped?" I relived that experience. Fear and panic would come, and I would deny and say, "No!"

The rape haunted me until I was in the twelfth grade. One day, a girl that I didn't know very well asked me, "Aren't you the girl who got raped in elementary school?" I said, "Yes, and what about it? How can this information help you?" The girl didn't say anything, and for the first time I felt free!

What has happened in your life that makes you feel like you are in bondage? What is the thing that causes you pain every time you think about it? What holds you hostage emotionally?

My ultimate freedom has come from my relationship with the Lord!

"So if the Son sets you free, you will be free indeed."

—John 8:36 (NIV)

You can be free!

Abortion

I was in college, I had a boyfriend, and I was getting ready to pledge a sorority. Then, I got sick. I went to the hospital and find out that I was pregnant! I had so many thoughts crossing my mind. I wanted to pledge. There was already someone who pledged another sorority and was pregnant. What was I going to do? What would my mother think? At that point in my life, God was not at the center. I felt like I was in a downward spiral.

My boyfriend at the time supported me in whatever decision I wanted to make. I decided to have an abortion. That boyfriend later became my husband.

We went to a place that was not near the college. I don't remember how I got the information about the location. This was in the 80s, we didn't have Google then.

I remember them calling my name. I went back alone. The doctor explained what would happen. I prayed and asked God to forgive me, then I put my hands on my stomach and told the baby I was sorry. I was somewhere around eight weeks pregnant. I realize now that I went into some form of depression afterwards. I didn't go to class. I felt empty inside.

I think that's why I ended up pregnant again. That time we got married. I would not choose abortion again.

Since then, I have told my truth and I have spoken to other women and women's groups about it. If you have been through abortion and feel guilt or shame, God can forgive you! Hold your head up high! Don't live in guilt or shame. You are not alone!

Breast Cancer

Since I lost one of my best friends to breast cancer about ten years ago, I always go to get my regular mammograms. She told me to go get a mammogram and from that moment I always did. The results were always the same—good. My breasts were normal; no abnormal findings. Not this time!

Around February 2018, I received a call from my primary physician to go back and get a second mammogram because apparently the hospital had been trying to reach me.

I went for the second mammogram and the doctor also did a sonogram. He came in to give me his findings. He asked me if someone was there with me. I said no. After all, at that point I had only moved to Texas six years prior. I had just moved my 87-year-old mother from Maryland and I still had a fifteen-year-old son to raise! I was also divorced by that time. I had three adult children, two of them were in other states. All of my family was in Baltimore. All of those things were racing through my mind as the doctor told me, "You will have to go for a biopsy."

While talking to one of my cousins and asking her to pray for me, she asked if I had spoken to one of her sisters who just had a biopsy of her breast and it was breast cancer. Another one of their sisters had a bilateral mastectomy two years prior.

I began to realize that God had a plan and a purpose even in this! My biopsy was scheduled for around 7:00 a.m. I was due in the hospital at 6:30 a.m. I got there at 6:15 a.m. The door of the women's center was not open yet.

The executive minister, my pastor, and my mentor all came to pray with me! We formed a circle in the middle of that waiting room. I felt the peace of God spoken of in John 16:33.

I went in and had the biopsy. I was told it probably would take up to a week to get the results. It would have been Good Friday by then. My cousin who recently had been diagnosed said, "You won't get the same diagnosis." I gave it to the Lord, praying that I wouldn't.

The next day at work I saw the hospital phone number come up on my phone. I went to an area where I could take the call. The doctor introduced himself; he was the doctor that performed the biopsy. He said it, "The result of your biopsy is cancer!" I felt numb. I was standing in the lobby of my office. I went outside. I didn't know what to do. I was in public, so I had to stay composed. I asked, "What's next?"

Oh God! What's next?! went through my mind.

I called my pastor and the executive pastor from church, went to see my mentor, and then I went to see my boss.

My mentor connected me with a friend of hers who had just completed radiation. She too had breast cancer. Remember I am not originally from Texas. I don't really know the doctors or hospitals here. I have a primary physician, yes. At home in Baltimore we have The Johns Hopkins Hospital.

God had a plan! The friend that my mentor told me about called me approximately 15 minutes after receiving my mentor's text. She told me about her breast surgeon and her journey.

Her breast surgeon was in my area (Texas is huge) and in-network for my insurance! Her surgeon became my surgeon. God had a plan! I found a devotional book that I received years before but did not use. The name of the devotional was *Be Still and Know That I am God!*

Between my mentor, my executive minister (who is a woman), young women from the Bible study I teach, and a young woman from work, I never went to a visit alone, except for the day I had to go to a specialist. My breast surgeon said she needed to be clear on how far the cancer had spread. The specialist confirmed that the cancer had spread throughout my breast and I would have to get a mastectomy. Did I hear her right?

God was still speaking to me. The specialist gave me a stuffed lamb named Faith! I went into my car after that visit with the specialist and cried. I was going to lose a body part! I never really identified myself with my breasts, but the thought of losing one really scared me. I called my cousin who had a bilateral mastectomy two years prior to get her advice. While I was sitting in the car crying and praying, one of my sons called me and asked did I order a t-shirt? He opened the package for me. The t-shirt said, "Be still, and know that I am God." Psalm 46:10 became my theme. During the journey, God also gave me the word joy! I saw joy everywhere! The joy of the Lord became my strength! Nehemiah 8:10.

Two of my adult children lived in other states. My daughter earned her master's degree in May. In June, I had a left breast mastectomy. My daughter and my oldest son moved to Texas to help take care of me and my mom. My middle and youngest sons were already with me. One of my nieces used all of her leave and came from Baltimore to take care of me.

For my reconstruction surgery later in 2018, one of my cousins came to take care of me. My middle son took off for three weeks. Remember I was concerned because I was by myself? Not so! My church family and my work family became my family! Even my middle son's coworkers brought food. My church family sent food. I had flowers and gifts. I had a village! I had the Lord! I was not alone.

In 2018, I had three surgeries in six months, and I am taking a chemo pill for the next five years because I still have my right breast.

Throughout my breast cancer journey, I was healed! Healed of the cancer, healed of the past, healed from how I look with my scars, healed! Throughout this journey, I became grateful for life. God gave me another theme or word and that is love! I learned to love me! I learned how to love God even more!

SOUL REFLECTION:

Rape, abortion, and breast cancer caused trials, trauma, and tragedy. All of those events could have ended in death, but God allowed it all to end in triumph!

I know God has given me His peace. No matter what trials, traumas, or tragedies you have gone through or are going through, God can allow you to live in triumph! God can give you His peace!

"And the peace of God, which transcends all understanding, will guard your hearts and your minds in Christ Jesus."

—Philippians 4:7

God will give you peace throughout the trials in your life. Trust the Lord and have faith in Him. He will make a way!

Don't get discouraged, the Lord has a plan for you. He will fulfill it. Stay strong and hold on to Him!

*"The Lord will fulfill his purpose for me. Your love, O Lord,
endures forever. Do not abandon the works of your hands."*

—Psalm 138:8

God has a plan and a purpose for you !

I Was Freed from My Virtual Bondage

MEKO KROUT

"Stand fast therefore in the liberty wherewith Christ hath made us free, and be not entangled again with the yoke of bondage."

—Galatians 5:1

When trying to decide what tattoo would be symbolic for my life, I chose a butterfly and roses. The major significance for me was the constant reminder of hope, which was the embodiment of spiritual growth and transcendence. A butterfly is symbolized in the Bible as the Holy Spirit that can transcend the ordinary and reach the heavens, and that beautiful rose symbolizes the ever-growing wisdom.

While going through the divorce process after twenty-five years of marriage, I hit one of the lowest points in my life. It was through the transition of being taken through the storms that I realized God had something greater in store for me.

What I realized was that during those 25 years of marriage, I was literally living in shackles. I had a tough time letting go of the past. They were the chains that were hindering me from loving myself wholeheartedly. There were also so many distractions, from technology to social media to my career, that it took me some time to come to grips with the fact that I had closed my ears and my heart to hearing anything God was saying to assist me in my healing process. However, God has a way of shutting you down and making you listen whether you like it or not.

I have been blessed to share my life story on many panels. My goal has always been to help others understand that no matter what you are going through or what you have gone through, you can reinvent your life after tragedy. For me, I never took the time to go into detail on how God put me in a position to really hear His voice.

When you go through a divorce, you want to take time away to reflect, relax, and heal. There are four stages that we each walk through in a major loss—grief, anger, acceptance, and healing. These four stages are all necessary.

Travel became my therapy. It was important to me because I hadn't gotten the opportunity to experience it with my spouse or family. We had been so focused on our daily hustle and bustle. But I promised myself that I was going to see the world. I made good on my promise to myself.

There was excitement in my spirit as I thought about how God was allowing little ole me a chance to experience the different cultures and people I didn't get the chance to experience while I was married. Yet, I began to feel guilty that I was traveling while my two youngest boys were at home. I struggled with really enjoying my time without them and my ex-husband. Something kept nagging at my soul and not letting go. My boys were adults and they were excited for me to get away and relax. I came to grips with the fact that I was unable to change the past. I had to move forward.

As the trip got closer, the anticipation that it was becoming a reality kept a smile on my face as I prepared. What kept running through my mind was going to the airport, driving to the resort, excursions, beautiful beaches, culture, and food that makes you gain ten pounds just looking at it. But there I was with my nose down in my work computer, books, and my phone; I missed out on reflecting and relaxing. My friends always said I was held hostage by work and social media, but I didn't listen. I can remember my resort butler saying to me, "You have virtual chains on." Of course, I really didn't understand what he meant at the time. He said to me, "God opened a door for you, and you are still held hostage to things." Again, I had a blind eye and closed ears.

As the vacation came to an end, it was time to return to reality. Our flight had a layover in Atlanta, Georgia, where we had to go through customs. As I approached the customs agent and handed him my passport, there was a slight pause as he checked the system. He asked me, "How are you doing? Did you have a good vacation?" In my mind, I assumed he was flirting. He asked me to follow him. Of course, I wondered what was going on. I was taken to a holding area and asked if I had any warrants out. I responded, "Of course not!" So, imagine my surprise when the agent said that I was flagged as a flight risk due to outstanding warrants and they were going to hold me over.

As they placed me in handcuffs and paraded me through the airport, it was the most demeaning and degrading situation I had ever been in. Especially as I walked past my sister and friends and no one could help me. I felt like I had hit rock bottom. While I was walking, I was in a complete daze. All I can remember from that moment was people staring and pointing as I walked by with my head down and tears flowing down my face. I kept wondering, *Why, Lord, is this happening to me? What did I do to deserve to be taken through this embarrassment?*

I assumed being paraded through the airport was embarrassment enough, but once we arrived at the station, the intake process was even more demeaning. Innocent or not, they don't care. I was fingerprinted, sent back to sit on the bench, called back up to answer questions, and then sent back to the bench. The process is grueling and time consuming. You can contact someone; however, my virtual bondage was taken away and I could not remember anyone's number. My saving grace was that my sister had me write some numbers on my arm while in the airport customs before they transported me to the jail in Atlanta.

An additional part of the intake process requires a quick check-up, a tetanus shot, and removal of all piercings. The correctional officer was very adamant about removing one of my piercings from the cartilage in my ear. As I mentioned before, this was the most demeaning process I have been through in my entire life. The nurse told the correctional officer that my piercing was fresh and new and shouldn't be removed. The female correctional officer yanked the earring out of my ear. You can imagine my screaming and the blood that was flowing from me. I probably was over the top, but at that moment the emotions that were so deep just began to flow from my heart. The intake nurse was so upset and showed me so much compassion. She had me come back to her office to help stop the bleeding and administer the shot. When I broke down in tears, she asked, "Why are you here?" I told her my story. Her words soothed the very essence of me that was hurting. She told me, "No matter if you committed the crime or not, God will take you through the storm. Trust and believe that He has better things in store for you." It was at that moment that I came to grips with the fact that God was allowing this to happen so that I would take a moment and listen to what He was saying. The intake nurse continued, "This is your shutdown and now you have no choice but to be still and understand what He is saying to you." She quoted Exodus 14:14: "The LORD will fight for you; you need only to be still."

As my communication with the outside world along with my dignity was being stripped away, I kept asking the question, "Why me, Lord? Haven't I been through enough for the last few years?" Looking around, there were so many women from all walks of life sitting in that holding cell. Some appeared to be strong and others were in a daze or crying, but at the end of the day they were all in their own space praying. I had to wonder what made me any different. But, in the back of my mind, I knew the Lord was taking me through for a reason. I just needed to sit still and listen.

When we were finally assigned to our pod, I was greeted by my cellmate. I honestly can't lie; I was terrified of her at first. She was a medium to large woman with her hair braided back into cornrows. She gave me the vibe of Queen Latifah in Set It Off. But you can't judge a book by its cover. She was the sweetest person ever. She showed me how to make my bed properly according to the system rules, how to clean our cell, and what to say and what not to say to the officers. She was a nurse who'd had an altercation with her daughter that landed her in jail. She too was worried about what was going to happen to her and her career as a nurse. My heart bled for her for all the turmoil she was experiencing with her children. We slept most of the time, wallowing in our own sorrows, not realizing how much time had passed.

A few days later, we were awakened by the correctional officers for all inmates to appear in court. The process required us all to line up against the wall in a single line, hold our head forward, and look straight ahead. You are not able to say a word to anyone. We were herded from one area of the facility to the next and put into another holding cell. They not only handcuff you, but they place shackles on your feet. When they got to me, I completely freaked out and asked, "God, really? You have got to be kidding me! How much more of this are you going to make me endure?" Because I completely lost it, the correctional officer thought it would be funny to put pink fur shackles on me. I tried so hard to make light of it at the time, but I still wondered, *Why me, Lord?*

As we entered the courtroom, I watched the judge deliver sentences on each inmate—whether they had time served, bail, or had to serve more time. After four hours of sitting in the courtroom listening, waiting, and anticipating what my outcome would be, I was the last person to be called forward. It wasn't what I expected; the judge advised that I couldn't be held as an Atlanta inmate and Dallas County had up to ten days to extradite me back to Dallas. All that kept running through my mind was my boys. Who would take care of them and feed them? And, would my corporate career be completely demolished?

Once we were escorted back to our cells after court, my cellmate asked if she could pray over me while preparing for her release. I had really lost hope in the short two and a half days that I was there, but I told her that I needed all the help I could get. While heading out, she left me with a quote that she said her mom always said to her, "Say a little prayer and trust in something greater than yourself." Again, I cried, cried, and cried some more. I cried more in those few days than I had during my whole divorce process.

For the next few days, I was basically in the cell alone; just the four white walls and me. I had no access to sunlight or any form of communication to hear the voices of my sons. It was extremely disheartening. The silence was so loud, I just wanted to scream, but all I did was cry. There came a time where days really felt like months. I didn't know if anyone was trying to help me or if God and everyone else had just abandoned me. The correctional officer's thought that I was the weirdest person ever since I was the only person in the cell, but I still chose to sleep on the top bunk. In my mind, that was the safest place. No one would mess with me if they had placed another person in my cell. I had self-inflicted bruises from climbing up and down from the top bunk and almost falling into the cell door.

My mind was all over the place. I was still not sitting still and giving my situation to God. I felt like a disobedient child being put in timeout. I finally got on my knees and cried out, "Lord, help me to open my ears and listen." I began praying and finally having a conversation with God. My understanding was truly bad and somewhere down the line our relationship got disconnected. I had been through so much disappointment and felt like my life was over. I prayed, "God, give me the strength and courage to speak life back into myself. I know I have a long road ahead once I am finally released. I need You to be my armor, my shield, and my confidant. I know somewhere I forgot about building a relationship with You. But today I am turning my life over to You, and I know that my storms will soon recede and blue skies are on the horizon. If You release me from the bondage physically and mentally, I am Yours."

Once I began praying, I started to just be at peace, realizing that everything is not in my hands but God's. On my fourth day, one of the ladies in our pod was kind enough to place a three-way call and contacted my family. I finally got a chance to speak with my sister. She informed me that they had found two lawyers to help me and I would be out the next day. It is so amazing how God works; everything just fell into place. He kept my boys' spirits high and I was able to speak to them and not fall apart. They wanted to make sure that I was okay and even joked asking, "Is orange the new black?" I couldn't help but laugh.

Day five was the day the correctional officer said, "Inmate Krout, grab your things. You are being released." I ran up the stairs in my pod fast to gather my items, which were only the mattress sheets, spork, toothbrush, and cup they provide during my intake process. I had never been so happy to finally be able to go home. I prayed and believed in Mark 11:24 (KJV) that says, "Therefore I say unto you, What things soever ye desire, when ye pray, believe that ye receive them, and ye shall have them."

Discussion

1. What in life is holding you back from hearing God's Word?
2. Are you allowing fear to put you in virtual bondage?
3. Have you embraced the embodiment of **spiritual growth and transcendence?**

SOUL REFLECTION:

I never really understood what it meant to release your fear of change, pain, worry, or issues and give it to God. I never once believed in saying a little prayer and trusting in something greater than myself. So, I continued to keep moving forward, but I ignored the signs that God was placing in front of me. He will allow you to have disappointments so that you will stop and listen to the message He has for you. My message was: "You have virtual chains and you need to step back and release them."

Even though I was broken, I am grateful for the experience. It gave me the will to fight. I'm so thankful for the storms. They gave me this testimony that I am compelled to share with others. I didn't know how, but I knew I had to share my journey in some shape, form, or fashion. Through everything, I am still smiling because He brought me out better than before.

We have to realize that there is life after tragedy. My story is no different from any other person's story. Everyone has experienced some type of storm and may feel like life is over. We have to speak life back into ourselves. Once we start, we will see God work and how amazing He truly is. We are not alone. We have to realize that our storms are placed in our lives to shower us for growth.

Self-Preservation for Servant Leaders

NECOLE MUHAMMAD

"Come unto me, all who labor and are heavy laden, and I will give you rest."

—Matthew 11:28

"Be careful what you ask for, you just might get it!" That is a famous phrase that I know all too well. But not without learning the power of "Be who you say you are," a phrase I learned from a phenomenal SoulCycle teacher from the Old Town community in Chicago, Illinois. See, on one end I have always prayed and shared with God my innermost thoughts, but I am just starting to learn how to consistently lay my burdens on Him and walk away so that I can get rest. Many believers will tell you they know what you are talking about, but not many believers will tell you that they really don't know how to do what you are talking about. I knew how to ask God for what I wanted, but once my blessings were granted and they became a burden, I did not know how to "be who I said I was"—a believer that had faith and gave God my problems to help me survive the intricacies of my blessings.

I am a servant leader in every area of my life. I am a wife and a mother. I am active in my sorority and other community organizations. I am also a former high school assistant principal, principal, licensed clinical social worker, certified life and sexuality coach, and a yoga teacher. Luke 12:48 states, "To whom much is given, much is required." That verse is easier to read than to experience. During an isolated seven years within my journey as a servant leader, I learned valuable lessons about letting go and letting God to really understand what was required. I was an only child with strong parents that instilled in me the value of commitment, credibility, responsibility, and following your word all the way to the end. Once I touched an assignment, it became a mission from God. I was told to always leave whatever I committed to better than I found it. That ideology became a way of life and ultimately the structure that helped to highlight my ability to lead and serve with unwavering compassion.

It was the end of October 2010. I made a decision that I wanted to do something bigger and different with my life. I told God that I wanted to transform lives, educate youth, and help make a difference in our community. For approximately six months, I sat in a first floor office as a school social worker and every day I would quietly take an allotted amount of time to visualize and focus. I was determined to make a difference with the children and adults I served in our inner-city community. I didn't specifically ask for a position, I asked for a mission. An unexpected financial event occurred, and I began to swiftly make plans to move away from what had been my norm for 17 years. Just as I began to say my goodbyes, the principal unexpectedly stated that she wished I had the credentials needed to fulfill an administration position at her school. After disclosing my credentials, I met the criteria for one of two administration positions she had to fill. Initially I was hesitant, but after clarification of the expected duties, prayer, and a conversation with my husband, I agreed with the strong belief that I received my mission.

Four months later without any barriers, I began my journey and stood in the hallways as one of the assistant principals in one of the most challenging high schools in the city of Chicago. My predecessor was a military man, strong, and unmovable. I had a point to prove, but no one was going to see me sweat. I was no stranger to the school, but the position required me to be out front and responsible for everything, which at the time was beyond my purview. Everyone expected me to have the answers, and if I didn't, I was going to find them. After all, I did accept the position and it was my mission. One day, I guess the stress of the new position caused me to complain and a community Bishop that provided services to our students looked me directly in my eyes and said, "When much is given much is required." I quickly shut my mouth and started to solve problems.

The summer was full of planning, long meetings, and hopeful outcomes. The first year was rough. I experienced tremendous personal and professional growth and as a team we made it happen. Doubts about my leadership ability decreased on the inside and the outside slowly switched from private corner conversations to productive face to face feedback. I knew I had a long way to go, but I made the necessary adjustments. I learned how to work with my adrenaline and sympathetic nervous system to stand tall with pride in my predecessor's shoes. I pulled a part of me from my core that I had never met to meet the expectations of my mission.

Then the unexpected happened on October 22, 2013. An altercation on the second floor of the school landed us on the international news. WTH! Security and staff intervened, the Chicago Police Department came in like a scene from a Quentin Tarantino movie, the school went on lock down, central office representatives arrived via FedEx, and the press was out and filming as 29 students were arrested and piled into law enforcement vehicles. There was no time to bend or break, just time to make sure it was handled like Olivia Pope on *Scandal*. The initial feedback from central office leadership was positive and surface, but less than 24 hours later everything turned upside down. I learned a big lesson about leadership and the inability to pass the buck when you are the one in charge. You must have all of the answers, and if not, know how to get them. I had been dipped in the reality sauce of servant leadership and making my word my bond.

For the next few months there were several serious meetings, changes, deep dives, follow-ups, and accelerated next steps for the school, students, parents, teachers, and community stakeholders to prevent something like that from ever happening again. However, within the first few weeks, additional altercations occurred along with other major unrelated incidents and the structure of a normal school setting still had to happen. Back to having it handled, I truly embodied Olivia Pope—knowing all the answers and never letting them see me sweat—but not without a paying a heavy price with my mind, body, and soul. I really need you to understand that in "my" handling it, I never went to God as a laborer with my burdens and sought rest. It had become ugly and every day seemed to get more challenging, but it was always handled. I didn't take the suggestion from 1 Peter 5:7-9 to "cast all your cares upon him for he cares for you. Be alert and of sober mind. Your enemy the devil prowls around like a roaring lion looking for someone to devour. Resist him standing firm in faith, because you know that the family of believers throughout the world is undergoing the same kind of sufferings."

As time passed, all I's were dotted and all T's were crossed with paperwork and the central leadership to make sure all stakeholders were satisfied with the unexpected and unfortunate snowball of events. But all I's and T's were not crossed with my mind, body, and soul. I developed a painful ulcer, began having issues with tachycardia (unannounced fast heartbeats), and sharp pains would shoot through my head. I also gained 30 pounds and began to withdraw from life. I was no longer an authentic people person; I gave my all at work and pulled from an unknown reserve of fuel to successfully complete each day. I sacrificed time with my family and friends and did not want to engage with anyone outside of work simply because I was burned out and needed to have time to handle it again the next day. I didn't care about the quantitative data that everyone wanted, I cared about the qualitative stories of the human beings that circulated through my halls every day and how I could use my influence and mission to help them live their best life. I was committed to the mission and for the next four years my multitasking skills increased 100 percent, but I lost myself and eventually came crashing down.

I wanted so badly to make God proud because it was never about any position, it was more about the mission for me to serve His people. See, I never ever wanted to be a principal of any kind, but the way the opportunity came it all made sense and the process was seamless. I love social work, helping and edifying people, and my experiences gave me access on a large scale to make a big difference. Throughout the endeavor, I would check in and debrief with God; but looking back, I never laid my burdens down. I held on to them while I had the conversations with God, never asking for Him to intervene in my affairs. Not because I thought I was God, but it didn't even cross my mind to ask Him to do something because I forgot about 2 Chronicles 20:15: "Do not be afraid nor dismayed because of this great multitude, for the battle is not yours, it's the Lord's."

A lifestyle change needed to happen, and I needed to save my own life! I began waking up early in the morning before everyone in my house, not to do work but to connect with God. I wanted to reconnect with Him in a visceral way that would allow me to absorb the lessons learned and begin to make decisions that were conducive to His purpose for me. I asked myself what worked for me in the past to help calm me, center me, and give me introspection. Yoga, reading, learning, and service lit up like a Christmas tree; so, I joined a yoga studio, began reading, and renewed my commitment to organizations that give me access to serving others. All three began to take over my life, so much so that I became a yoga instructor, my Kindle and Audible are full,

I gained additional certifications, and several times a month I am heavily engaged in service. I also joined a gym to help me lose weight, resigned from my job as a principal (took a hefty pay cut), went back to social work, and I spend a lot more time with family and friends. I learned that I had several untapped skills, I work effectively under pressure, I am a true servant leader, I love helping and edifying people, and I cannot do it in a silo or without God's help.

Self-preservation is mandatory for you to be used effectively for God's purpose. Your mind, body, and soul work in tandem to help you show up for His assignments. As a servant leader, you must stay connected to God and take care of yourself as you are proof of His omnipotence, omnipresence, attributes, grace, and love. There are several questions that I asked myself throughout the healing process and road towards self-preservation. The main question I have asked myself is: "Who did you have to become to do what you have done?" This question gives me insight into my untapped strengths and also allows me to see how far or close I am or was on the path during my journey. I am committed to being intentional about my communication and alignment with God in everything I do. I want God to be pleased with His daughter, and I want to live a purpose driven life and never lose myself again trying to do it all by myself. It is not meant for us to burn out, struggle endlessly, and walk our journeys alone. Fully embrace Deuteronomy 31:6 as it reminds us to "Be strong and courageous. Do not be afraid or terrified because of them, for the Lord your God goes with you; he will never leave you nor forsake you." May God be with us all!

SOUL REFLECTION:

Not quite sure who said it but, "Everything happens for a reason." Everything about this entire experience pushed be closer to God and introduced me to parts of myself that I never knew existed. To be created in His image and His likeness is to be aware that there is nothing you can't handle. It is also important to be aware that you must seek God when you believe you are tired or have lost your way. Without Him everything is impossible.

A Fine Line Between Purpose and Pride

NINA WHITE-HODGE

"For I know the plans I have for you," declares the LORD, "plans to prosper you and not to harm you, plans to give you hope and a future."

—Jeremiah 29:11

As I sit here, I can't help but to reflect on my past and more specifically my past mistakes. Now let's be clear, I am a completely faithful believer in Jeremiah 29:11, God having a plan for my life. I don't think understanding that God created me for a specific purpose was ever a problem. In fact, I've always been one who believed wholeheartedly that I am the favorite of God. Not the favored, but the favorite of God. I knew God loved me and always would. My problem was never about purpose, I was confident in that. My problem was pride and the intermingling of purpose and pride. It has taken me a long time to make a distinction between the two.

Don't hide your story. Know your history to understand your present...

Many will agree that these two words, pride and purpose, are so far apart in meaning that it would be impossible to get them intermingled. So, the million-dollar question is how on Earth did these too terms get intermingled in my life? I was born a premature, four pounds, three ounces baby girl. I don't believe my issues with pride really started at that point, but as a premature baby I did learn how to fight early in life. Many bad habits started from a significant maybe even traumatic event that occurred in someone's past, so let's fast forward to second grade. I would like to point out that I believe this is the space in time where an event happened that absolutely changed the trajectory of my entire life. When I was in the second grade for the second time (yes, the second time), I had an incident where I was severely cut on my face in the middle of my forehead. My brother Christopher was swinging an old table leg like a bat and struck me right between the eyes. One millimeter to the left or right and I would have lost an eye. God saved my eye, but I was left with a huge scar and gained the new nickname, Scar Face. Later that same year, my parents divorced and that impacted me a lot. Prior to those two events, I really wasn't that great of a student. At least I don't remember being a great student, hence the reason I was in the second grade for the second time.

I quickly discovered my ability to control one thing, my education. I controlled whether I did good or bad, and I was celebrated for it. I became so good at it that doing well was expected. Doing well with my education was so highly celebrated that it began to bleed over into the rest of my life, including my everyday decisions. I gained the "goody two shoes" title and I was pretty proud of it. I didn't care. I was trying to be good and the fact that people noticed was frosting on the cake. I didn't realize it then, but there is an aspect of pride that formulates even when you attempt to be good. I had to learn that even being good was not good enough. God was not interested in my goodness; He was interested in my surrender.

In my teens and young adult years, I participated in the community choir in our small town. While others my age were out dancing and partying and having a great time, I was at revivals singing. I was at church but still got home the same time as my classmates who had gone to the club. I felt that was ok because of where I was and what I was doing, so I did not respect my mother's rules to be in the house by a certain time. My gifts were developing but so were some really bad habits. I had a genuine belief that I was using my gifts for God and pursuing His purpose, so everything was okay.

Don't hide your story or blame others, own it!

Throughout my young adult years many things occurred, but it was always clear that God had His hand on my life. I was nervous about everything but never afraid of anything. God blessed and expanded my gifts with every turn. Every downturn seemed to be wrapped with a bow and silver lining. It was clear that all my gifts were growing but so was my pride. While pregnant with my first child, things got so bad at one point that I was living in an abandoned house eating PB&J sandwiches. One phone call to my mother could have changed my situation, but I chose to stay there. I didn't want anyone, especially my mother, to know my living conditions. So, I did what I felt all good Christians do at a low point in their life... I went to church... well, revival. It was a great experience. The evangelist spoke over me saying everything was going to be alright and my baby was special and anointed.

Just as she said, life did get better. I was able to get into a low income one-bedroom apartment. There wasn't much in it, but it was home and most importantly I was excited to share with everyone the blessing God had given me. I had managed to get past living in an abandoned house and sleeping on the floor without anyone knowing. In my mind, that was the major blessing. Not only did we get an apartment, but a lady across the street gave us furniture. I didn't get out much, but I continued to sing at church. I met a lady who played the piano at church and she lived in the same apartment complex as me. Her apartment was beautiful and always clean. At that time, I was struggling with keeping my little one-bedroom apartment clean. Ms. Piano Lady came to my apartment and helped me clean up and get everything in order. It was SOOO bad. I was a new mom, and there was trash everywhere. If it wasn't trash, there was dirty clothes and clutter. Once again, I hid it from my family and friends. Ms. Piano Lady was persistent and refused to accept any of the many excuses I gave her. Once she was inside, she did not judge me; she worked with me to get my house cleaned and kept clean. Keeping it clean involved me making a list of things to do, doing them, and checking them off. Ms. Piano Lady was a true blessing, I learned a lot from her; unfortunately, it was both good and bad things. Making ends meet financially was a little tough each month. I stretched the food stamps, AFDC, and WIC benefits. While shopping, Ms. Piano Lady showed me how to "run checks."

Before the networks and internet, it took three days for a check to be cashed against an account. We would make a purchase, wait three days, cash another check, and deposit the money to cover that check. Then in another three days, we would go and cash another check to cover that check. That would continue until we received welfare checks. Each check cost 50 cents to cash. Here I was a new mother, choir member, maintaining a clean house, and running checks. In the beginning I was covering anywhere from five to fifteen dollars. But before I knew it, that amount was two to three hundred dollars. There was a $50 check cashing maximum amount for each store. I spent hours running to four or five stores to cover the incoming checks. I remember praying and asking God to please deliver me from that mess. I didn't take responsibility for my actions. It felt better to blame it on the Christian piano lady who dragged me into that sin. I never said anything audibly, but in my heart and mind it was her fault! God fixed the mess. The banking system upgraded, and check satisfaction was applied instantly. One minute I was floating checks and the next minute I was in court on a worthless check charge. I didn't receive jail time. God really showed me favor. I stopped it and never talked about it to anyone. I paid my restitution and moved on.

Don't hide your story, take responsibility for your role in its creation!

There were more peaks and valleys, but I could not complain. Despite everything, God was still blessing me. With two small children, I relocated to Orlando, Florida, with my cousin. God soon blessed me with an apartment, a car, and a career all in the same day. Later, I was reacquainted with a childhood friend I had not seen since junior high school. When I first moved to Orlando, I had a dream about the encounter. In the dream, this friend was my husband. I was in awe that a lifetime had gone by and I was seeing my friend. There were some red flags, but I overlooked them. As far as I was concerned, they didn't apply in that case. God would fix everything, and He did, just not how I expected or wanted Him to.

We were together for 18 years. He adopted my daughters from my previous marriage, gave them his name, and raised them like his own. He bought a home for our family and my first ever brand-new car. Later we purchased a second home, moved into that home, and rented the first home for additional income. We opened his dream business. Both of us worked full-time in corporate America and part-time in our small business. It was not long before we were doing very well financially. We decided to—well, I decided, my husband just went along with it—sell our homes and build our dream home. There was nothing we could not accomplish working together. To look at us by the world's standards we were successful. We lived in a gated community, our kids went to private school, God blessed us to have another daughter, I was attending law school, I received a job promotion, the business was doing well, we were active at church, and we spent time fasting and praying together. From the outside looking in we had everything. We were "the perfect family."

Then it started... our home that had increased in value to be worth almost $500K was now worth what we paid and was decreasing daily. Corporate America was also downsizing, and my husband was one of the workers affected. Orders were slowing down at the business. After using our savings, we transferred the girls from private school, and I began maximizing student loans to pay bills. Long before we ran out of money, my husband suggested that we pull the kids out of private school and cut back on spending. I felt that the private education was important, and I thought what we were going through would turn around soon. I didn't want people to know the hardship we were in.

There was another issue that existed prior to our marriage that had been left unaddressed. As long as we were doing well it was unaddressed; however, when the pressure became overwhelming, I was not interested in supporting or encouraging my husband. Every time he mentioned the finances, I brought up his issue. As far as I was concerned, we were doing fine and could have mustered through if he would just get another job and get rid of his issue. It was not long before we just stopped talking to each other about it. I felt that since I worked, made all the money, and paid all the bills, he couldn't tell me what to do financially. Maybe he felt that since I wanted to wear the pants and lead, I should carry the financial load. My best friend from second grade was now my worst enemy. The saddest part was that to our family and friends we were still "the perfect couple."

I hid everything! I would ask my co-worker to give me a ride to work because of car problems, but the reality was I just didn't have gas in the car. The clutter from my past resurfaced in the worst way. Now it wasn't a one-bedroom apartment filled with garbage it was a two-story, five-bedroom house in a gated community. I was doing everything to hide what was going on. I felt that my husband was refusing to help me and was doing everything to make me fail, but I wasn't having it. I was going to force him to get a job and help me. I made a conscious decision to stop paying the mortgage. I started spending on things I wanted. I had gas in my car, I was able to go to lunch with my co-workers, I hired someone to clean my home, I started a small skincare business, the girls could go to after school events and field trips. Everything was paid except the mortgage. I figured I would show him. But things didn't get better, they got worse. The bank foreclosed on the house.

The atmosphere was toxic, but to the public we were holding tightly to our "the perfect couple" title. However, people could see that everything wasn't all good in paradise. "The perfect couple" was falling apart. Over the next few years, the downward spiral continued, and we hit rock bottom hard. I realized we were in trouble, I just didn't realize how much trouble, nor did I want to accept how much my pride had to do with it. It took the death of my brother, the exposure of the inner workings of our household, and a move to Dallas, Texas, to cause me to see ME in the MESS.

SOUL REFLECTION:
Never allow pride to disguise itself as purpose. I always knew God had a specific purpose for my life, that wasn't the problem. The problem was that I was driven by pride, not purpose. My story is filled with rape, failed BAR exams, divorce, and prison, but it continued to restoration, recovery, and renewal only after I surrendered and God reprogrammed my mind. Today I am just as, if not more, accomplished and successful as I was then; but this time, I have things in the right perspective. Look for my new book, *I'm Not Sure I'm Ready to be Me*, to get the full scoop on how God took all this mess and more and turned it into a singer, songwriter, fashion designer, author, actress, judicial reform advocate, attorney, business owner, executive producer, and yes, a wife again...only this time, purpose driven not driven by pride.

A Letter to Her

RONI BENJAMIN

*"For I know the plans I have for you," says the LORD. "They are plans
for good and not for disaster, to give you a future and a hope."*

—Jeremiah 29:11 (NLT)

*Little girl, I see you hiding. No need to hide anymore. I
remember you and I know who you are. Let's take a journey
together. Are you ready? No, oh, I understand. You need
me to address what happened in the past first, huh? Well,
ok... let me start by saying you're not to blame. It's not your
fault your daddy left. You were only two years old. Daddy
and mommy just couldn't get along. Believe me, with their
horrible tempers, it was best. They would've killed each
other before long. So, somebody had to leave. Imagine being
raised by strangers because your parents were dead or in
jail. See, they merely did what was best for everyone. You are
not at fault for a worthless man's behavior. He hurt you and
took advantage of your innocence, Baby. He violated your
body and jeopardized your life. I know you're asking yourself
several questions, "Why didn't I tell someone sooner? Was it*

because I was ashamed? Did I fear retaliation? Is it because he threatened me and my family? How will I ever trust again?"

Beautiful girl, you were afraid and didn't realize what was happening to you. You were only six years old... still a baby. You were still learning about life, your surroundings, and the elementary things. There are people in the world who make bad decisions all the time. They don't think about who they hurt with their choices. Your brother didn't realize you would forever be scarred by his actions either. Sweetheart, you were eight years old when he made you touch him down there. I know the truth. I saw it all. But you thought it was better to keep silent to protect him, right? Save him from going back to yet another group home, away from the family. See, look at your heart. At such a young age, you put the needs of others above your own. This is a noble quality, Baby... when it's used for those worthy. I'm going to tell you something that I want you to always remember. What's done in the dark will always come to light. As you grow older, don't protect someone who is causing you harm, Baby Girl. They'll do it to someone else. Imagine another little girl going through what you went through? Would you want her heart and body to hurt like yours? I know you wouldn't. I love you so much. I feel your presence every day.

Roni, you are a good girl with a good heart, and you will heal from those events. You did not do anything to deserve what happened to you. You are stronger than you think, and I will protect you for the rest of your life. I will speak for you. I will be loud so God will hear me from the heavens. I will fight for you so you'll never have to fear any man. I will console you when the nightmares return. I will remind *you of the good memories of your youth to make you smile. Do you remember when cousin Michael would throw you in the air and catch you every time? How about the time you raced Mommy down the grassy hill as you both wore red and white to match? Do you remember the soft hugs and kisses from your grandma after a long train ride on Metro North? Oh, how those cinnamon raisin bagels from Grand Central Station were the best.*

You are so special because you're YOU. The one thing that nobody else has is YOU. Your voice, your mind, your story, your vision. So, let's build, play, and dance more. Let's draw, write, and live as only you can. You are not alone, and you can trust me always. We have to finish what we came here to do. Write our way out!

The letter I wrote to my younger self was the turning point of my life. I gave myself permission to forgive, not just myself but others who brought pain and suffering into my life. The shell of the woman that had lived in the shadows for 30 plus years was now filling up her soul with love, hope, and a strong desire to pursue her dreams and live to her fullest potential. I remember the day I was prompted to write that letter. I met a phenomenal woman, Latoya Haynes, who is a human resources business partner and certified life coach. I knew after our first introduction that she would be my mentor, but I didn't know how impactful she would be in my journey. During our relationship building moments, she'd give me practical exercises to do on my own. The first was to take seven minutes to write out my greatest accomplishments to date and take a few more minutes to celebrate them. That exercise was the most challenging, believe it or not. I sat down night after night for a week straight and stared at white pages, at a loss for words. After fighting through humble beginnings, winning dance competitions, rocking runways all across New York City, and raising two amazing children, I felt I had nothing noteworthy to consider as an accomplishment. On the seventh night, I cried like a child in a broken state. Yet, I was determined to fight through that defeated state of mind and dig deep to find moments of my life to be proud of. Before I knew it, the list grew longer and longer. Here are a few of my achievements that I wrote down:

- Qualified for the finals for the Colgate Women's Games at Madison Square Garden
- Survived depression after my first brother's death in 1995
- Finished high school in spite of dealing with my brother's death
- Qualified for the final round of auditions for the Atlanta Hawks cheerleaders
- Qualified for the semi-final round of American Idol
- Received the Sales Leadership Award from SunTrust Bank and was awarded a free trip to Disney World
- Received several achievement awards from employers' year over year
- Raising two respectful children
- Completed a pharmacy technicians certification with honors
- Started and built a lucrative adult entertainment business
- Purchased a home on almost two acres of land
- Planned a destination wedding in Destin, Florida

- Started a new technology business within the travel industry
- Motivated and inspired others to reach their fullest potential in life
- Mentored teammates
- Helped develop the new customer concierge role
- Remained friends with several people from my youth
- Served on a panel to share life experiences, feed hope, and inspire middle school students

As I wrote down each accomplishment, I felt a sense of pride flow through my body. They reminded me of the huge milestones that I'd never celebrated. It was then that I realized I needed to pat myself on the back for overcoming obstacles or conquering challenges more often, which also revealed that I needed to create more celebratory instances in my life.

The other exercise was to write a letter to my younger self and tell her anything I wanted her to know from the adult version's perspective. Six-year-old Roni needed to know that the goodness in her is still in me. I was to read it aloud then burn or tear it up. After writing "A Letter to Her" and reading it out loud, I knew that I could not destroy it. I had a feeling this letter would connect with so many other people. I felt that I could be the voice of the voiceless, the powerful for the weak, and the strength for the brokenhearted. Above all things, I finally released the bondage of my dark past that held me back from success in multiple areas of my life.

Pains from my past were jeopardizing my chances for a happy present and fulfilling future. I didn't realize how the events of my past shaped the way I felt and interpreted the world. Living through abuse from childhood and feelings of abandonment can leave wounds on your mind that affect your mental and emotional health throughout life when they are not addressed. The Robert Wood Johnson Foundation noted that an estimated 44 million adults live with a mental illness, yet nearly 60 percent don't receive treatment in a given year. Most of the time, it's because they don't recognize that their traumatic experience is negatively influencing them. That was certainly my case. You see, I was raised to "Take a lickin' and keep on ticking" and I believed that "What doesn't kill you only makes you stronger." Both are true; however, if those lickins' are so traumatic that they shake your very existence, it's mandatory to heal those wounds so they don't become permanent scars.

There are many opinions and definitions of trauma. One thing that is absolutely true is that trauma is an experience that threatens one's sanity, bodily integrity, or life. My traumatic events were child abuse, abandonment, death of my brother, domestic abuse, and a near death experience. Unbeknownst to me, those events affected how I forged relationships with other people. I was depending on others to fill a void in my life in one capacity or another. I did not realize certain behaviors, thoughts, and emotions were directly related to my traumatic experiences. Trusting others was complicated because it required me to be vulnerable. That was, and at times still is, difficult because of a past where my trust was violated and abused.

Through my soul repair process, I noticed a connection between a history of past failures and my lack of trust which ultimately fed depression, low self-esteem, and kept me from completing the things I started. The next phase of this vicious cycle was regret. We all know that regret can rob you of happiness when you dwell on past mistakes that were made, things you wish you had done differently, or scenarios where you felt you did everything right but it still didn't work out. Well, I also learned from the most successful people like Les Brown, Johnny Wimbrey, Cheryl Polote-Williamson and others that failure is part of the path to success. Any kind of meaningful self-improvement involves failure. Only exceptionally lucky people manage to get everything right on the first try with no challenges. Most people who succeed will try something, fail, and then use what they've learned to avoid that pitfall again as they pursue the next endeavor. Do these words resonate with you? "I wish I would have done this better. I wish I wouldn't have made that choice. I wish I would have made better choices." Well, you didn't. Wishes won't undo the past. At some point, we have to make the decision to stop letting regret control us, so we can enjoy the present and work towards a better future. No one else can do that for you. You have the power to change your future. And you probably have more strength than you realize. Letting go of past hurts and regrets will keep anger from filling up your heart, mind, and soul. The problem with anger is that it can easily poison all of the good and positive things in your life.

For years, anger created walls and boundaries that felt impossible for me to overcome. A distinct characteristic of being angry for me was that I didn't listen to find a solution. Instead, I was more interested in having my emotions validated. The real problem started when anger kept me from healing. Let me tell you something about anger, it can create tunnel vision when we feel we are right. We will demand that we be heard because we believe that we deserve to have our pains addressed! Well... I quickly learned I can't hold on to that anger forever, otherwise it'll eat away at my mental and emotional health. I learned that anger itself is not productive. It can be fuel to a fire, but anger won't do the work that is necessary to actually make a change. What anger is guaranteed to do is upset one's peace and derail happiness. I choose to find inner peace and joy. Working with some amazing people, life coaches, and mentors taught me that in order to find inner peace, I must understand that I will only find it by working hard at fixing the problems and making better choices. You see, no one else can do that for you. The pains that sabotage your present and future are often rooted in past wounds that require professional help. I know that all too well, because I had to overcome my own poisonous past and mental illness to reach my happy, peaceful present. Thank God for resources such as Employee Assistance Program (EAP) with my employer, psychologists that take their role in our lives very seriously, and life and transformational coaches that commit to our healing process. If you are unhappy with your life or feel that your past is keeping you from the future you want, talk to a qualified mental health professional. That's what they're there for. They make the process of putting your pieces back together much more efficient.

Over the last several years, I've been on a journey of healing and forgiveness. I started with me. I forgave myself for holding on to the pain from the past and forgetting about the great memories that shaped who I am. I forgave myself for all the counterproductive decisions made over the years.

I've forgiven my father for the decisions he made in the past that affected my upbringing. I forgave the guy that attacked me at age six and the woman who lied to protect him. I forgave my brother for his ill practices against me as a child. I forgave the man that shot and killed my brother. I forgave the guy that left my brother to die alone on the pavement in Astoria, Queens. I forgave the men who broke my heart and trampled on it with unfaithfulness, violence, and disrespect. Next, I remembered the promise I made to my younger self in the letter to her: "... you can trust me always. We have to finish what we came here to do."

Soon after the start of my soul restoration, I found the courage to pursue acting, writing, and speaking. I played a car expo attendee and party goer in the hit TV series, *Queen of the South*. I had a lead role in the award-winning stage play, *Soul Purpose*. I also played a pastor in my very first movie, *Black Diamond*. I'm in love with the concept of creating a real story for a character and making it relatable to my audience. Writing allows me to express my feelings and ideas in my own words. There's such a liberating freedom that comes with this creative expression that's unmatched. Public speaking and delivering a strategic message is a beautiful process as well. In a world of social media and electronic devices, we forget sometimes how important social connections are. Face to face engagement, human touch, and conversations are essential in building lasting, sustainable, and healthy relationships. Through each talent, I found my life's mission—to uplift and inspire others to live their best life.

SOUL REFLECTION:

Through the growing pains of my life and the refining process, I realized God has always been with me. I've learned to trust Him with every ounce of my being. When I have more months than money, I trust God with my finances. As I raise my children and things appear to be in disarray, I trust God to guide me and help me instill good morals and values into them. I throw every anxiety onto God Himself to sort out so that I can focus on my mission to uplift and inspire others around the world.

Healing Through Self-Care - Turning Grief, Fear, and Pain into New Energy

RUBY JEANINE BATISTE

"Create in me a pure heart, O God, and renew a steadfast spirit within me."

—Psalm 51:10 (NIV)

The clock struck midnight and I was beyond excited to see and experience life in 2012. I anticipated that the new year would be much like 2011 in many ways, but I was eager to celebrate life. 2012 would be a special year to me because, God willing, I would be celebrating my fortieth birthday.

January and February were filled with busy days of my typical routine which consisted of my career duties as an educator, my wifely duties, my motherly duties, and spending time with my social circles. The months of March, April, and May tend to be more hectic due to the nature of my career as a public school administrator. I also suffer from extreme spring allergies, so I am typically physically exhausted during those months, as well.

Late March and early April were preparing to change my typical way of life forever. My younger sister was involved in a car accident towards the end of March 2012. Her car was heavily damaged, but she walked away with minor physical injuries. I was so thankful to God that she was okay. My "perfect" family was still intact. My family was "perfect" to me because all of our immediate members were alive, and we truly loved being around one another. I was blessed to grow up in a loving Christian home with a father and mother who loved each other.

They poured so much love into creating a home for me and my younger siblings. I was so blessed to have them both here and healthy. My sister has a heart of gold and was busy with her career and community service projects. My brother was the youngest of the family. He and his wife had the honor of bringing the first two grandchildren into our family unit. They were high school sweethearts who married in their early twenties. They were such a joy to be around. As for me, I had been married for five years. My husband and I have one son who was three at the time. He was our pride and joy! My "perfect" family was the essence of my spirit.

Towards the end of March, I wasn't feeling well on a consistent basis. It was more severe than my usual springtime allergy battles, accompanied with fatigue. While at work, I was visiting a school campus when I started to feel extremely weak and sluggish while walking. I decided to stop by the nurse's office to take a short break. The campus nurse asked me how I was feeling and suggested that she should check my blood pressure. She checked my pressure three different times. She had a very concerned look on her face and informed me that she was going to call an ambulance to transport me to the hospital because my blood pressure was extremely high, it was at stroke level. I convinced her that I was okay to drive myself. I immediately left her office and drove to the emergency room. The emergency room staff monitored my blood pressure for four hours. It was still extremely elevated. To my surprise, I was admitted to the hospital for a three day stay.

While I was in the hospital, all I could think about was how concerned and afraid my three-year-old son and husband looked when they came to visit me. I began to realize how short life is and I thanked God for giving me another chance to treat myself better and to spend more time with my family. My mother and father were also relieved that I was okay and that I would now be under a doctor's care to treat my newly diagnosed high blood pressure. Our "perfect" family was still together.

Three days later, on the morning of April 4, 2012, our home telephone rang. My husband answered it as he prepared to leave for work. I was still getting dressed for work. He walked into our bedroom and handed the telephone to me. I assumed it was my mother because we would often converse on the telephone early in the morning. My father and I would often converse during my mid-day breaks at work. He shared motivating, encouraging, and humorous experiences with me when I needed them the most. I asked my husband who was on the telephone and he stated it was my younger sister.

I took a deep breath before I greeted her because she was not calling at her usual time and she rarely called my home telephone. She shared some very unexpected and illogical news with me, which immediately brought me to my knees. I cried out in a scream, "Not the baby!" My younger brother was dead! He died right before he and his wife were about to wake up to start their day. He died of a heart attack. The paramedics pronounced him dead at 6:30 a.m. He was thirty years old.

My brother was an amazing husband, father, son, brother, cousin, and friend. He had just called me the night before to check on me and to lecture me about taking care of myself. I had just seen him a few months earlier when he brought me some medicine because I had fallen ill while I was working out of town in Austin where he lived. Now, he was dead. My sister-in-law and young nephews experienced him dying in their home. The baby of our "perfect" family was dead. I asked God, "How could this be? How could the baby be the first to go?" My "perfect" family was no longer perfect. We experienced a devastating loss that hurt beyond measure.

The process of laying my brother to rest was long due to the initial shock everyone was going through, especially his wife. Easter weekend was also coming up, so we chose to wait until the following weekend to lay him to rest. Of course, death wasn't anything new to our family, but it was the first time we had to let go of an immediate family member. My parents had to bury their child. My sister and I had to bury our younger brother. My sister-in-law had to bury her high school sweetheart, best friend, husband, and the father of her two precious young sons. I was nine years older than my brother. I experienced my mother's pregnancy with him and his birth. I watched him grow up. I was blessed to experience so much of his life and was proud of the family man he had grown to be. There was no celebration in my heart regarding his homegoing. My heart was shattered.

Time stands still for no one. Life was still happening months after my brother's passing. I still had to be a wife, mother, daughter, sister, friend, boss, and an accountable colleague. I was paralyzed in grief and fear. I was sleep deprived because I was afraid to go to sleep at night. I thought I would die, just like my brother died. There were so many days that all I could do was cry. I would put on my make-up, dress-up, and try to be the best version of myself for those who needed me, but I was so broken on the inside. I was physically there, but emotionally unavailable and disengaged. I was spiraling out of control and missing out on valuable time with those who were still here on Earth with me.

I had to pray and fight for my life. I couldn't live for God in the state I was in. I knew I had purpose for still being here, but I was bound by fear and grief. One year after my brother's passing, I was starting to climb out of the dark space I was in. I had done pretty well masking the pain I was going through in public. Our family was slowly beginning to accept God's will for our beloved, who we felt was gone too soon. My mother and father were in pain, but their faith walk was so strong. We were getting used to our new normal. Our family never stopped worshiping, praising, and loving God. Fifteen months after my brother's passing, my loving father died.

"Lord, God, why is Daddy gone too?" I would consistently ask God why. We need Daddy so much. My mother needs him, my sister needs him, my nephews need him, my son needs him, and I NEED him! "Lord, God, why are you willing this upon my family?" We laid my father to rest in

August of 2013. I was a true Daddy's girl who had nothing but love, respect, and admiration for my father. Even though I didn't want to let my daddy go, I knew I had to. I knew he suffered from a broken heart too when my brother died. He was a man of God and a man of few words. He kept himself busier than usual before he fell ill in May of 2013. My mother said he stayed busy to fill the void in his heart. I was so much like him in many ways.

The following months were filled with many sleepless nights because I fell back into being fearful. I was operating on three hours of sleep per day. My blood pressure was consistently high due to lack of sleep. I was busy worrying and not busy living my life as God had intended for me to live it. I couldn't handle being around people; crowded places were the worst. I just wanted to stay in my room with the lights off, but that wasn't an option. The marriage I prayed so hard for when I was single needed to be nurtured. The four-year-old son I was blessed with needed his mother. I had a great career, family, and friends who also needed me to be the best version of myself. January 1, 2014, was on the horizon. A new year was on the way and I promised myself I would trust God and rest in His perfect peace.

My new normal now consisted of me taking courses towards my doctorate degree. My sleep pattern still hadn't improved and the doctoral courses were adding more stress. I truly thought the pursuit of the doctoral degree was where God was guiding me.

One Saturday morning in February of 2014, I clearly heard God tell me, "Go make the lotion." He told me, "Go make the lotion," every Saturday morning that February.

But, I did absolutely nothing because I didn't understand what He was telling me to do. The only experience I had with oils and butters was when I experimented with them on my hair, since I decided to stop relaxing it with chemicals in 2010. I'd never made lotion and why would I go make lotion when I can buy it at the store?

On the last Saturday of that February, I received a phone call from one of my sorority sisters who I highly respect for her faith walk and her business skills. I hadn't spoken to her in months and we didn't converse regularly. Upon exchanging pleasantries, she asked me to make her some lotion so that she could sell it when she went out to vend at various events. I was blown away and totally silent! I hadn't told anyone what God had been telling me to do for the past month. I knew that my response had to be yes. God was asking me to trust Him. After I said yes, I asked her one question, "Out of the thousands of people you know, what made you ask me to make you some lotion?" Her response was, "I don't know, it just came to me."

I was stagnant for a few more months because I was trying to figure out what God was instructing me to do. Every Saturday during that time period, God was telling me, "Go make the lotion." His prompting was clear, and I knew it was Him because my pastor taught a sermon in 2011 that resonated with me. Through his sermon, he taught us how to discern when God is directing you to do something. He taught us that God's prompting is very persistent and will not go away until you do what He has directed you to do.

On October 6, 2014, I was finally obedient to what God had been prompting me to do since February of 2014. I made my first batch of lotion and used the excess oils to make a sugar scrub. I was amazed at how good the lotion and scrub felt on my extremely dry and eczema prone skin. I took what I made to work the next day to get some feedback from some of my co-workers. I was blown away by their responses. They wanted to purchase some for themselves after trying it! My response was, "I am not selling this. I made it for one of my friends." Their response was, "Well, we want some too!" I've had consistent orders since I did what God directed me to do.

On November 8, 2014, I launched my online website for Custom Blends by Nine Bath and Body Products LLC. God gave me the name of my business which is also part of my middle name. Nine stands for Now Inviting New Energy. By being obedient to God, He introduced me to a world of self-care that I didn't know existed. I experienced so much joy when I created my products. I felt better than I had in years when I would mix and fulfill orders. The aromas from the oils gave me new energy and were part of the healing I needed after the passing of my brother and father.

I eagerly enrolled in classes to learn more about skincare formulation, soap making, and candle making. I utilized social media to meet and collaborate with people who shared tips and strategies regarding skincare formulation. I also expanded my social circles by vending at various events.

My skin is the best it has ever been because of the nurturing quality of the products I use when formulating skincare products. I found joy in pampering my family with handmade products. I continuously share my story of how God saved me by giving me Nine. I've helped other people fall in love with the skin they're in and have taught them to use relaxation products as part of their self-care too. I no longer live in fear of sleeping at night and have renewed my heart, body, and spirit by letting go and promptly being obedient to God in all things.

SOUL REFLECTION:

Once I listened to and acted on God's directions, He healed and blessed me far beyond what I could have ever imagined. I delayed my healing by being disobedient and stagnant.

The Whispering Voice of God

DR. SONJA V. BROWN-DELOATCH

"And he said, 'Go out and stand on the mount before the Lord.' And behold, the Lord passed by, and a great and strong wind tore the mountains and broke in pieces the rocks before the Lord, but the Lord was not in the wind. And after the wind an earthquake, but the Lord was not in the earthquake. And after the earthquake a fire, but the Lord was not in the fire. And after the fire the sound of a low whisper."

—1 Kings 19:11-12 (ESV)

Over the last year, I would describe myself as being in a fog. You might ask, "Why a fog?" I say fog because it forms when the nights become cool and long. It is a mixture of cool temperature and increased humidity that forms a dewy presence. I would say that I have felt like that many days. I view those nights as cool and long, almost like a spiritual occurrence of God with a dewy presence. Fog is the formation of many cool, tiny droplets of water (moisture) that mix with the humidity close to the ground at night and shows itself in a very dense morning. Fog is no more than a mist of vapors that rises up with a dew settlement at night then lifts or stands still in the early morning; it moves, it covers, it grabs hold, it hovers and slowly disappears as the day begins. I am at a place of calmness and I am no longer afraid of the morning fog.

Like the dew in the morning, gently rest upon my heart.

My fog is lifting, and the recall of my childhood has begun to haunt me. Issues that I felt were resolved are still there. A sense of loneliness hovers over my head and heart. The question that lingers each waking moment is, "What's next?" While I have one of the greatest opportunities in life, which is to write and publish my story, I still find myself in a fog most days as I think about who will be affected by my truth.

I had to surrender all. Yes, I surrender all.
All to Thee, my blessed Savior, I surrender all.

I am the middle child of a family of five siblings from my parents' union. For years, this middle passage left me alone in thoughts and ideas about who I am. I never felt true love from my mother, and my oldest sister hates me. Why? Hell, I do not know. At this point in my life, I really no longer care. I have always known that my three brothers, my grandmother, and my godparents loved me. Even more than that, I knew God loved me then and He loves me now.

Yes, Jesus loves me. Yes, Jesus loves me.
Yes, Jesus loves me, cause the Bible tells me so!

"Jesus Loves Me" is one of the first songs I learned in Sunday school. I love to sing. When I was young and things were not going well for me, I would go to the one bathroom in the house and sing my little heart out. My mother would yell, "Girl, if you don't get through in there and stop all that singing!" Then, I would whisper and still sing. You have to understand, I was being disobedient. Yes, I was. I needed an outlet. I needed a safe place and I needed to know I was loved. Through the music, I could hear the whispers of God's voice.

Sometimes I feel like a motherless child
a long way from home.

The songs I would sing were old negro spirituals, and I love a great hymn. I would call on God to come and take me far away from the circumstance of this life. There had to be a better place for me at five, six, seven, ten, and fifteen... even if it was in the bathroom of our home. I knew there was a better place and God was going to take me there. I was going to be alright. I could hear the famous lyrics whispering, "Precious Lord, take my hand, lead me on, let me stand... Take my hand, precious Lord, lead me home."

When I was a young teenager, my mother put me out of our home. I had gotten into an argument with her boyfriend the night before. I heard what sounded like a slap. I knocked on my mother's bedroom door. It was unlocked, so I went in. I saw my mother sitting on the edge of the bed. I asked him, "Did you hit my mother?" She looked at me and said, "It's ok!" I said, "No! That is not ok! I am not leaving." He got angry and he left the house. *The fog again.* I cannot for the life of me remember where my eldest sister or my three brothers were. The next evening, he came back to our home and into my brother's bedroom where I was sitting on the lower bunkbed. He called my name. I ignored him. He said, "Don't you ever talk to me like that again." I looked at the television like I did not hear or see him. Oh, I did not tell you that once he left the night before, after he and I argued, my mother asked me to leave the house. I asked her, "Where am I going to go? I don't have nowhere to go, Mama!" My mother then said, "You are not going to mess up my money and things I need." Then I said, "I can walk around this house like he is not even here." Thinking about it now, that was impossible. There were three bedrooms, a living room, a kitchen, and a pantry all on one floor. I had no idea what I was going to do.

The next day I told him, "Don't talk to me, get out of my face, and leave me alone." I stood up to get out of the room. He was six feet plus in height and over 200 pounds, and I was less than 49 inches and weighed 135 pounds. He started choking me, and I was afraid! I could see my father's golf trophy on my brother's dresser drawer, and I heard two voices. They were whispers from the evil in me and the good in me. Praise God, the angel of good never picked the trophy up and hit him on the head. I would have killed him! The God of protection removed me from his hands and Mom put me out!

Hold on, keep your hand on the plow, hold on.

We (meaning black folk) did not talk about suicide, we just did not do it. We were taught from the good preacher that suicide is a sin and you would go straight to hell if you killed yourself. If you took your own life, you had no way of asking God for forgiveness. Understand that at that point, I just did not care what people thought about me. The people in the flesh were not there for me, so taking my life might have been a plan. But, taking the life He created was not an option. I am just crazy enough to believe that even in the moment of despair, when you want to end your life, God our Father comes and whispers in your ear.

Hold on just a little while longer, everything will be alright... How great thou art.

I had become a fighter at that point. My mother had put me out of our home, I moved to a friend of the family's home for a couple of weeks, and then my mom allowed me to return to her house. It was no longer a home for me. I worked that summer to prepare myself for college. During that first year of college, life for me was no better at my mother's house. I finished that semester at TSU and transferred to MTSU in Murfreesboro, Tennessee. I had moved to the town where my sister was in college. I was happy. I thought we would have a relationship. We had the same Mom and Dad. We were raised in the same house. That was a hope and dream that was only in my head. I stopped singing but never stopped praying. I made new friends, attended classes, and I was even in a class with my sister. One day my sister did not come to class. Our classmates asked me, "Why are you here, I thought your mom was having surgery?" I had no words, just pure anger and embarrassment. I called one of my friend girls, got wasted, and cried myself to sleep.

Nobody knows the trouble I've seen.
Nobody knows my sorrow.

The semester ended and I had not done well enough to stay for another year. I moved to Georgia and stayed with my father and his family for less than a year. My godfather had died, and I wanted to moved back to Nashville, Tennessee. I was hoping I was going to build a relationship with my mother. Mother's Day was coming, and I was missing her. I was also missing my grandmother and my dear friends who had been there for me. When I left Tennessee, I never told anyone where I was going, I was just going. I had hoped to see my mother and fix our relationship. As I sat to type this out, it amazed me just how much of my life during those formative years is still in the fog. I stayed with a friend girl that I knew in college and slept on her floor. I never consider myself homeless, but I was. I recently heard that my own daughter considered herself homeless for a short time in her life. She had completed college, transitioned to another city in North Carolina, and secured a place with a friend girl. The relationship did not work out and she found herself on the street. She did not tell me or her father. I would have tried to fix it for her. While I understand her struggle, I never put my children out. To a fault, I hovered and covered them too much.

I don't remember how long it was before I got on my feet. I worked different jobs, from preparing boxes in a factory to packing ice on a salad bar. I was determined not to be a hooker, I was not going to sell drugs, and I was not going to sleep around. That was not the plan for me. I believe that during those years, God was covering me. After about three months, I got back into school and started taking business courses. I worked during the day and took classes at night. I would catch the city bus from one end of town to the other.

I started going back to my home church in north Nashville. One Sunday morning after church, I went to my grandmother's house. I knocked on her door and she broke down crying. She called my mom Nunny. "Nunny never told me where you were. Baby come on in," she said. From that moment on, I have always been in.

Coming on in the room; Jesus is my doctor and
He writes out all of my prescriptions, He gives me
all of my medicine in the room!

Whispering questions, whispering thoughts, and walking in God's authority

1. Do you find yourself in a fog of life?
2. Have you allowed yourself to explore if there is something in that fog that is holding you back?
3. What methods have you used to help you get out of that fog?
4. Prepare a place for yourself to have your whispering moments with God.
5. To hear the whispers, take time during your busiest moments to stop and clear your head.
6. Know that you are never alone; God is always with you.

Glory, glory, hallelujah! Since I laid my burdens down... I feel better, so much better. Since I laid my burdens down.

SOUL REFLECTION:

If you are looking for me, I will be gone. You will find me underneath the Tree with my hands stretched out touching the hem of His garment so that I can be made whole.

This place you are going everyone cannot go. We know of the devastations that happen in this world. Oh to be kept by Jesus! God created us in His image not ours. We are just merely passing through this barren land. Make room to explore beyond what you see, what you have heard, and what you know. If you allow the things of your formative years to hold you hostage, you may not allow transformation to take place. You want to continue to move forward in this world called life. Do not allow anyone or anything to have power over your actions. Only God can order your steps. "Ain't gonna let nobody turn me round... I'm gonna keep on walkin', keep on talkin', marchin' into freedom land."

Beginning to End: A Journey to God

MARIE HART

"Once you were alienated from God and were enemies in your minds because of your evil behavior. But now he has reconciled you by Christ's physical body through death to present you holy in his sight, without blemish and free from accusation."

—Colossians 1:21-22

Growing up, I wished there was a manual that told us what to expect as we got older. I also hoped that we could turn back the hands of time or push a button to restart the day or year. But since that is not the case, I've decided to help guide someone who may need it even, if it's just one day. Each year, I wrote in a journal all the things that happened to me and how I felt during that time. I hope my journey empowers and teaches us that our time is short on this earth. We should love hard, get closer, and care about each other now because we are not guaranteed tomorrow.

Teens—The Beginning Years

I got the best job in the world at a tech agency doing what I love—working with computers. And the better thing was that my parents were God-sent. But, like most teens, I wanted to do things all on my own because I knew everything. There is nothing worse than a teen that knows everything. At some point, that brilliant mind of mine would tell me that what my parents were telling me was right and of course I was wrong. At 19, I had a good job and was still trying to find myself after the end of a long-term relationship. I was free and could date and be with anyone I wanted. I didn't need my mother to tell me what to do anymore; there were some things I needed to accomplish on my own. We got into a huge argument and I left home angry with her, never to return. They say that once you've lost time you can never get it back. I wish I had listened.

The Early to Late 20s—The Learning Years

I thought to myself, *Living on my own with strangers is not working for me. There are times when I have no money for gas (so I drive slowly in hopes of conserving the amount that I do have). This life is not for me. Why can't I chuck it up and go back home to my parents' house? Because then my mother will say, 'I told you so.'* So instead, I stayed put and continued going to school and finally working. One day as I was coming back into town, I wanted to meet up with one of my high school best friends. In doing so, I ran into a man that would become my daughter's father. Not soon after that, I found myself pregnant by a man that not only had another woman pregnant (I found that out later), but who cannot help but stray to other women. I turned to my father who I believe knows everything and he said, "Marie, boys will be boys. Stop looking for boys and let the man find you." Of course, I didn't believe my father and I loved that man, so I stayed. I was fighting for that man and doing drive-bys (on him) and lookouts for him. I did not care or understand that when a man loves you, following him around and doing things out of your comfort zone is not the way to keep him. And ladies, having a baby won't keep him either.

I was in love, he loved me, and no one could tell me otherwise. But what man who loves a woman has another baby by a woman outside of his relationship, while going to another woman's home to be with her? All while I am sitting at his house waiting on him to come back. Yes, I was flawed, but at 20 with a good career going what can I say? There was no one there to tell me not to do it. And my girls all thought that he was the best. He knew just what to say and how to make me feel, so why would I turn away? I had that man's baby and he would love me forever. At least that was my train of thought. But, he didn't have two pennies to rub together and he lived with his mother. So what could he provide for our child and me?

I soon had to quit my job because the doctors thought that I would no longer be able to work. So with my tail between my legs, I went to my parents. And of course, like the good parents they are, they took me back in. No questions asked. But, of course, my mother had a lot of opinions on me being pregnant. As she should; she is a mother. Soon I was doing it on my own and I found another job. The father of my child couldn't even pick up medication that I needed for our child that I was carrying (medicine that was already paid for) because, of course, he was out swimming and enjoying life. At night, I cried. This could not be real; this was not how I wanted my life to turn out. Of course, this too shall pass.

My mother invited me to go with her to a longtime friend's daughter's wedding. I didn't want to go because I was big and fat, because I was pregnant, and I didn't want people to see me. But if you know my mother, you know that she will bother you until you do what she wants you to do, hence why I love her so much. So, I got dressed to go to the wedding. While there, we were sitting at the table, a slow song came on, I looked up, and coming to our table was a man that I had not seen in years. A man that I had been with for seven years. Seeing him again made my heart flutter, but I felt so ugly at that moment. He was not the person that I wanted to see at that time. I weighed over 200 pounds. Why would he want to see me? My mother and her friends were all looking at him and smiling at me. He came directly to me, and while still looking at me he said, "Hi!" I looked at him and said, "Hello." What an idiot, "Hello." Really??!! He then said, "Marie, would you like to dance?" I thought that was the sweetest thing. But even though I wanted to dance, of course, I said, "No." So he took my hand and to the dance floor we went. We danced and continued small talk. Me against him felt right.

My heart was pounding, and I was afraid that he could feel it as well. As the music wound down, it was almost as if we could not bear to part. I knew the moment we locked eyes that we would be together again. He asked my mother if he could take me home and she said that was fine. So, we left and went driving after the reception. We talked for a long time and found out that we both missed each other very much. Weeks and months went by and everything was going well. Then tragedy struck his family, and things changed for us. Not too long after that, we stopped seeing each other again. Then, my beautiful baby girl was born healthy and happy. My daughter's father stayed out of the picture. Sometimes we would talk on the phone, but it was nothing major. My heart told me that it belonged to him even then, but he was still seeing other people anyway so why should I care? Years went by and finally, after losing some of that baby weight that would not go away, I was able to enter the military when my daughter was two years old.

Early to Late 30s—The Adult Years

Right before entering the military, I started dating an older gentleman that I thought would treat me better because he was older. Of course, that man was controlling down to the clothes I wore and the food that I put into my body. The good thing though was that because of him I lost a lot of weight. During my trials, since I was no longer living at my family's home, I realized that it made me want to be on my own. I wanted, no I needed, to be independent. There was something inside of me that wanted to show my mother that I could do it on my own. During that time, I met a lot of guys.

And since I wasn't seeing anyone, I was having fun. While I enjoyed my time away from being a mother, I also missed being around my daughter, so she came out to stay with me. Then, I wanted to go home and so did she.

At this time, since I had moved out of my parents' home, I stayed with my brother and his wife and kids. The younger gentleman was such a great friend and was so caring toward me that I soon would look to him for more. He would stay outside to ensure no harm would come to me. I guess being a woman made him err on the side of caution.

As time went by, we started to become the best of friends. There were days when I could not wait for him to come home so that I could see him, so the other guy and I broke up. I wasn't willing to give up being friends with the younger guy to be with the older gentleman. So, my friend and I got closer, staying up late to talk. Then one day I kissed him and ran. While on my girl's trip, I realized that this younger man would be mine. So upon my return home, I told him how I felt, and he felt the same way. A few months later, I left for the military and thought that I would not see him again. On my return home from training, he proposed to me, and I was so excited to say yes! We moved in together once I got my duty station and I got pregnant a year after that. Those times were trying for us. In the beginning, we were learning about each other and it got hard. I didn't like how he was doing things or even how he cleaned things; it irritated me to the bone. Also, I felt that since he wasn't working and I was in the service, he would do the housework. But that didn't happen.

After a while, I became enraged, threw things, and cussed him out. He remained quiet. Then, it got to the point where we were fighting and drawing knives on each other. Finally, our neighbor called the police. They came over and spoke with the both of us. A couple of days later, the landlord gave us an eviction notice. I told her the situation and she allowed us to stay as long as we made sure that it never happened again. That day was a learning day for me. After going through this very embarrassing episode—in public, might I add—we learned that I was pregnant with twins. But five months later, tragedy struck my new little family, and our babies were stillborn.

Nothing in this world could have hit me as hard as the death of my babies. It was almost like God was punishing me for all the bad things I did throughout my life. So for that, I lost faith and my world was shattered. Even the man that stood beside me through that time was lost to me. I felt that there was no way he could understand how I felt. Finally, after the loss of my stillborn babies and twelve miscarriages, I had a beautiful baby boy. I still felt the loss of my babies, and I felt that my anger was justified as no one took notice of how I felt. The military advised that I go to anger manage-ment, but I couldn't talk to a stranger. How could they know how I felt? Soon after having my son and returning from leave, my contract with the military ended and I went home. But I knew that I did not want to go home with my son's father. I needed time to myself because I had spent time with someone else since I was a teen. I needed time away from everything.

Tragedy would strike my family again when we found out that my father had stage four brain cancer (*Glioblastoma multiforme*). It shook my world. I had spent all of those years away from my family, living life and not knowing how sick he was, and now the time was gone. Those years could have been spent making memories with him.

I fell in love with a married man who didn't want me. He just enjoyed the idea that he could have me whenever he wanted me. I was a convenience. I felt stupid because I should have listened to the same advice I had given my friends. Never once did I think of God or pray to Him throughout that time; I was still angry. I found a new job and met a Godly woman who told me to come to her church. So I did. It opened my eyes, and it was almost like God was in the church saying, "Welcome home."

40s—The Understanding Years

Going to church the few times that I did throughout the years did nothing to help me. I was lost—so lost—that I felt that nothing would save me. Soon, though, I would learn to understand and trust the journey that God has put me on. And that no matter what, God would always be walking right there beside me. I still have bad days, but those days aren't as bad as the ones I had when I was not walking with God. Today, each struggle is a little bit easier to bear. And even though I have a lot of tears, God is always here beside me to wipe them away and shed some light on those dark days.

SOUL REFLECTION:
Understand that our scars serve a purpose. They remind us that we were broken but we have survived, and that God's unfailing love is always there holding and sheltering us. We can never turn back the hands of time, but we can learn from the mistakes we make and grow from them. With everything that I have learned, love is ever present in my life with God.

Sources

About the Authors

Nwanye Davis-Barnes is a survivor of abuse and trauma who is convinced that God is real! Being a single mother in her 20s, she quickly realized that faith and education would be a ticket out of poverty for her and her young son. While working alongside top executives, Nwanye swiftly adopted the belief that "we are required to give the same level of respect to the janitor as we would the CEO." By all accounts, Nwanye was not supposed to make it this far.

I understand that my life's journey (as difficult as it has been) was to prepare me for now.

Nwanye holds a bachelor's degree in business and currently serves as the executive chief of staff to the CEO of a professional sports organization. She has been married for 12 years to her husband Damon. Their blended family has blessed them with three children: Dayah, Wan'Ye and Damon-Alexander.

To connect, email her at Nwanye.Barnes@gmail.com

Tyreese R. McAllister has over 25 years of experience in emergency mental health, helping individuals experiencing both crisis and traumatic events. Tyreese is a doctoral candidate pursing a Psy.D. She is a member of Delta Sigma Theta Sorority, Inc.

While serving her community and developing her career, Tyreese balanced her life with her beloved family. She and her husband of 28 years, Anthony McAllister, have two beautiful daughters, N'Daja and Ayana. In March 2017, Ayana was killed by gun violence while home on spring break from college. The McAllister's—having lived a life of public service and ministry—triumphing over tragedy, founded The Ayana J. McAllister Legacy Foundation, a non-profit organization whose mission is to engage minority communities disproportionately impacted by gun violence through advocacy and education strategies. It is their intention to significantly reduce incidents of homicide, suicide, and acts of violence resulting from irresponsible use of firearms by dangerous individuals.

Learn more at www.ayanamcallister.com

Ladda Hawkins is a single parent of two sons living in the Dallas, Texas, area. She is a certified special education teacher and employment interview coach. Her diverse upbringing as a biracial child within the military community influenced her passion to be creative and embrace a globally minded perspective of learning. Her hobbies include reading personal development blogs, moderating social media groups, and connecting with the educational and entrepreneurial communities.

Ladda's personal initiative is to help working parents cope with workplace trauma by developing connections with their God-given gifts and abilities to view work as praise. She mentors and trains homeschooling parents to become virtual marketing assistants for online businesses.

An avid volunteer, Ladda has supported organizations aligned with child welfare and disability advocacy, crisis intervention, minority businesswomen initiatives, and educational technology committees for access and equity in public schools.

To connect, email her at info@laddalove.com

Angela T. Kinnel is a 13-year veteran educator, ordained minister, bestselling author, and public speaker. Her passion is to encourage, motivate, and educate the world about Jesus Christ and their identity in Him.

Angela earned a bachelor of science degree in agricultural economics from Fort Valley State University and went on to pursue a master of science degree in the same area at Tuskegee University. She obtained a master of arts degree in education with an emphasis in curriculum and instruction and is also a 2017 graduate of World Changers Bible School where she earned an associate degree in Christian studies. She is currently a candidate for a doctor of divinity degree. Angela has co-authored three anthologies to date.

A native of Dawson, Georgia, Angela currently resides in the metro Atlanta area and is a member of World Changers Church International in College Park, Georgia.

Learn more at aktheauthor.net

Crystal Cunningham is an inspiring personal development coach, speaker, and author. She's an unstoppable go-getter, dedicated to helping others become "Crystal Clear" in their life purpose and vision. Relatable and down-to-earth, she has also acquired a 19-year tenure with one of the top Fortune 500 companies within the telecommunications industry. Her powerful message of hope combines with her life experience to empower and encourage people everywhere.

As the CEO of Crystal Clear Communications & Consulting, Crystal has hosted a variety of forums for women throughout her community. The many trials and tribulations she experienced in her youth including teen pregnancy, being a runaway, abuse, and addiction developed her into a true woman of inspiration. Crystal is helping others gain courage, confidence, and clarity in their own lives. Her first book, *Rise Up In Hope*, encourages readers to live in their power and freedom to have a "Crystal Clear" life.

Learn more at www.CrystalCunningham.com

Jacqueline L. Shaw is a native of Oklahoma, born in Clearview, Oklahoma. She is the oldest of five children. Jacqueline attended Wetumka High School then later attended Seminole Junior College. Jacqueline is the founder and CEO of Flower Mound Child Care Professional Association and the director and owner of Shaw Child Care where she directs the everyday business responsibilities of a licensed home daycare.

Jacqueline is a member of the Lewisville Child Care Association, the First3Years organization, Texas Registered and Licensed Childcare Providers, North Texas Home Daycare, Christian Daycare Providers, Women of Flower Mound Club, Flower Mound Women in Business, Denton County Democrats, Flower Mound Women's Business League, Democratic Women of Denton County, and Denton County Texas Association of Black Democrats.

Jacqueline has three beautiful daughters ages 26, 23, and 21. They are currently residents of Flower Mound, Texas. She volunteers with North Texas Food Bank and the Greeters Ministry at Westside Baptist Church.

To connect, email her at jacquelinelshaw3@gmail.com

LaSonja S. Campbell's professional passion is rooted in people development, performance, and building strong cultures. She was the first African American female to rise through the sales ranks at the number one biopharmaceutical company in the world to earn the regional business director role, leading a multimillion-dollar business of sales professionals.

LaSonja is a graduate of Florida A&M University where she pledged the Beta Alpha Chapter of Delta Sigma Theta Sorority, Incorporated. She is an active member of Triumph Church in Detroit, serving as the youth ministry lead. She is also the youth program director for The Torch of Wisdom Foundation in Southfield, Michigan. She is a warrior and advocate for children while carrying the torch for love!

LaSonja is married to Darryl E. Campbell. Together they enrich the lives of their godchildren: Derrin, Zuri, Connor, Lyric, Briana, Ashley, and Julian along with their grandchildren: Jackson and Maya.

Learn more at www.campbellsoulm8s.com

Derrick L. Faggétt is an accomplished motivational speaker, life coach, and self-made serial entrepreneur. He has built a successful network of like-minded individuals which has afforded him a passive residual income while he sleeps. Derrick is passionate about creating a healthier legacy for his family. More importantly, he values what he is leaving inside of them spiritually.

Derrick is an original founding partner of Maximizers Wealth Builders LLC which promotes the importance of ownership and financial literacy. Defying the odds of all statistical data that states he should've been dead or incarcerated, he is a living testimony that anything is possible when you're living for your dreams instead of fighting for your limitations.

Derrick believes in his heart that it is his purpose through his related experiences to teach, resurrect the family order, inspire, and encourage men to step up and into their rightful roles as kingdom men.

To connect, email him at derrick.faggett@gmail.com

Sharon R. Clinton is a follower of Jesus, an experienced speaker, dynamic producer, mentor, and coach. She has served in several leadership capacities for over 20 years, most recently at One Community Church, in Plano, Texas. She believes it an honor to help create platforms of expression, with cultural relevance that challenge the lens of perspective and make room for others to lead authentic lives.

While her personal story is no secret to those who know her best, she hopes her transparency and triumph over sexual assault, domestic violence, and emotional and physical abuse will compel others to denounce the lies of a dying world opening doors to God's healing, grace, and truth. As an empath with a passion for people, Sharon now serves as a change agent and servant leader in her role as a deputy executive director in the mayor's Office of Community Empowerment and Opportunity in Philadelphia.

To connect, email her at sharon@sdrobinsoncompany.com

JoLanda K. Harris is the founder of Liv On, LLC, a cancer and major illness coaching practice. She is a cancer coach, author, and speaker. Her mission is to empower others to redirect their purpose while living with a major illness.

Diagnosed in 2017 with breast cancer, JoLanda faces the challenges of ongoing treatment with courage. Her resilience in the face of adversity inspires others. This is reflected in her no-nonsense, straightforward, yet humorous style.

er JoLanda was born with a strong sense of purpose, positivity, and the passion to lead. She is a graduate of Alabama A&M University and an active member of Alpha Kappa Alpha Sorority, Inc. She has more than 15 years of experience leading women entrepreneurs in building sustainable client relationships. In addition, she spent nearly 30 years as an auditor with the federal government.

JoLanda lives in Huntsville, Alabama, with her husband Andre.

Learn more at www.LivOn1.com

Dretona T. Maddox, RN, PHN, LCSW, was motivated by hardship. She survived homelessness as a teen stifled by life and was forced by circumstances to abort her first child at age 15. She crushed all of her adversity and went on to earn her bachelor of science in nursing from University of Phoenix and her master of social work from University of Southern California.

Maddox's challenges were the catalyst to her life's work. She is dedicated to trailblazing as an in-demand public speaker, a Teen Parent Advocate™, and the founding executive director of Purposely Chosen, Inc., a non-profit organization that provides support and advocacy services to pregnant/parenting teens in foster care, that includes two maternity homes in Southern California.

Working for over 25 years as both a nurse and nurse social work practitioner, Dretona balances her love for impacting lives with supporting her husband of 27 years, Keith L. Maddox, a family of six, and three beautiful grand-children.

To connect, email her at dretona@dretonamaddox.com

Cynthia Fox Everett is a mother of four and a grandmother of seven. She is a U.S. Army Veteran of fourteen years. She has an associate degree in criminal justice and furthered her education at Shaw University. Cynthia rededicated her life to Christ in 2003 and accepted the mission and the responsibility to serve in the house of the Lord. She wants to empower and inspire others to seek Jesus and find the strength to heal so that they have courage to rewrite their future, tell their story, and help others heal.

Cynthia is a certified life coach and a multi-bestselling co-author of Amazon's *Souled Out* and *Soul Talk, Volume II*, with Cheryl Polote-Williamson as the visionary. She is also a bestselling co-author with visionary Venessa D. Abram, MBA, in *The Voices Behind Mental Illness, Series 2*. She is a member of NAMI, an advocate for domestic violence, and a survivor.

To connect, email her at cynthiaeverett8@gmail.com

Damita Jo Crosby is a motivational speaker, evangelist, author, entrepreneur, wife, and mother. She is devoted to the task of helping women know themselves and flow in transparency. Damita Jo founded and directed Reuben's Clean and Sober Living, a California 501(c)(3), and for over 30 years she has been involved in women's ministry. She was licensed as an evangelist by the Church of God in Christ in 1997.

Her debut book, *Sanctified H.O.T.T.I.E.*, promotes positive body image. Her message of positivity out of negativity is also expressed in *Don't Get Comfortable in Shallow Water* and *You Ought to Visit Grandma More Often* (co-authored with celebrity chef Andre' Carthen, releasing in spring 2020). This is Damita Jo's second literary work with the Soul Movement, the first was *Soulful Prayers* (released in June 2019).

Damita Jo currently resides in Dallas, Texas, with her husband and son. Together they serve in ministry with an emphasis on building marriages.

To connect, email her at DamitaCrosby@yahoo.com

Janis Barnes is a facilitator and life coach who speaks and ministers to women's groups. She has a prayer and devotion ministry and is a breast cancer survivor who recently started a breast cancer support group for breast cancer patients, survivors, and their families.

Rev. Barnes has a bachelor of science degree from Coppin State College and is a member of Alpha Kappa Alpha Sorority, Inc. She has worked for 7-Eleven Inc. for 18 years as a certified business consultant, zone merchandiser for fresh food, and now as a corporate learning specialist.

Rev. Barnes is a second-generation preacher in the African Methodist Episcopal Church. She is a member of the ministerial staff at Smith Chapel AME Church in Dallas, Texas, where she teaches the young women's Bible study.

The daughter of the late Benjamin and Rev. Martina Madden, Rev. Barnes is the mother of four children: Eugene III, Jordan, Jasmine, and Ian.

To connect, email her at Favored46@gmail.com

Meko Krout's life motto is "Rise above the past and kick the presents a.." A mother, author, producer, activist, and creator of A.I.N., Meko Krout has made it her mission to help guide women through personal changes such as divorce, loss of a loved one, or becoming an empty nester. Her life changes led her on a new path as a "Pure Living Architect."

Meko is best known for her brand A.I.N., an altruistic project of fashion, art, and business

which allows accessory designers to showcase their designs in front of fashion forward judges along with the exciting opportunity to create or increase visibility for their product line.

In 2018, Miko published her first book, *A Family Blinded*. When she is not working on her brands, she is busy working full-time as a VP and Automation and Test Support Manager, NAACP ACT-SO chair, and president of the Dallas Development Network.

Learn more at www.mekokrout.com

Necole Muhammad has over 25 years of experience in a variety of fields that provide direct service to marginalized communities, at-risk individuals, and holistic services. She is a certified overflow coach, licensed clinical social worker, yoga teacher, certified sex coach, clinical trauma and compassion fatigue professional, and a former high school administrator. Necole is also the executive director of Urban Social Worker & Associates 501(c)(3) and she teaches four different types of yoga through Soul of Namaste, LLC. She has been married for 23 years and has two adult children.

Necole received her undergraduate degree in law enforcement administration from Western Illinois University, master of social work from Chicago State University, master of educational leadership from American College of Education, and currently all but her dissertation from Capella University for a doctorate in social work. No matter where her career has gone, helping people thrive has always been at the center of Necole's work.

To connect, email her at necolemuhammad@yahoo.com

Nina White-Hodge is a native Floridian who was born to Philip and Wanda White in Winter Haven, Florida. She is an actress, singer/songwriter, mentor, speaker, fashion designer, executive producer, attorney, and author. Her priorities start and end with God, having ministry with family tucked in the middle. She has a wonderful husband, Jay; three beautiful daughters: Anastasia, China, and Ephria; and, a handsome grandson, Mo'Ziah. Her special passions are empowering women and believing in a balanced and fulfilled lifestyle encompassing all aspects of a woman's physical, mental, emotional, and spiritual wholeness.

With 23 years of experience in corporate America, Nina uses her bachelor of arts in business and her juris doctorate in law while serving on the board for Dress for Success Dallas and P50F. She also serves as a mentor for AT&T Women in Finance. Nina has her own non-profit organization, 117 King & Queen, through which she advocates for judicial reform and the wrongfully incarcerated.

Learn more at www.theninawhite.com

Roni Benjamin was born in Queens, New York. The younger of two children, she was raised in Astoria Housing Projects by a young single mother. At a young age, Roni was exposed to drugs, molestation, and murder which later led her into a lifestyle of promiscuity, self-doubt, and emptiness. Her writing gives insight into how she endured the trials of being a mother at a young age, broken heartedness, domestic violence, and her search for true love. Her beautiful children, Corey and Summer, became her reasons to live full and persevere.

Through determination and a renewed mindset, Roni awakened her inner superhero and has taken her life to new levels. As a Toastmasters president, she develops many members into effective public speakers and leaders. She now walks in her purpose as an entrepreneur, actress, author, radio personality, and speech coach. Roni has a deep desire to inspire others to reach their fullest potential.

Learn more at www.ronimbenjamin.com

Ruby Jeanine Batiste is a servant community leader who is committed to helping all individuals enhance the quality of their life. She is a professional public school administrator, with over twenty years of experience in the Texas public school system. She earned both her bachelor's and master's degrees from Texas Woman's University in Denton, Texas. After a series of life changing events, Ruby answered a divine call of entrepreneurship in 2014, which led her to start making her own relaxation and personal care products. She is the founder, owner, and operator of Nine Bath and Body Products, LLC, a published author, and an educator.

Family is truly the essence of her soul. Being a wife to her husband, Ivy Jr., and a mother to her son, Joshua, has become one of the greatest passions and missions of her life. She and her family reside in Ovilla, Texas.

Learn more at www.customblendsby9.com

Dr. Sonja V. Brown-Deloatch, a woman with great faith and fortitude, has been referred to as "The Singing Preacher." She currently works as a licensed social worker in Murfreesboro, Tennessee, and provides services to Veterans who suffer with mental illness, substance abuse, homelessness, and Post-Traumatic Stress Disorder (PTSD).

Sonja is also a trained chaplain; senior pastor of Winters Chapel African Methodist Episcopal (AME) Church in Lebanon, Tennessee; proud member of Delta Sigma Theta Sorority, Inc.; and, a member of Order of the Eastern Star, the Association of Clinical Pastoral Education, and the National Black Chaplains Associations. Sonja completed her undergraduate degree, master's degree, and divinity school at Shaw University. In May of 2018, she became the first woman of the 13th. Episcopal District of the AME Church to be confirmed with a doctor in theology from the historical Payne Theological Seminary.

Sonja has two adult children and enjoys her time being Oma to her two grandchildren.

To connect, email her at sonjavbd@gmail.com

Marie Hart is a single mother of two and a United States Navy Veteran. While on active duty, Marie received the Navy and Marine Corps achievement medal for performing commendably during her routine responsibilities and achievements. Marie is also the owner and founder of Signature Paralegal Solutions and Nannies with Hart, a nanny service that helps families and single parents that cannot afford to send their children to the daycare center. Marie is currently working on building the foundation HopeTogether. A foundation whose belief is that "together we can do anything if we care enough to do it together."

Marie believes that with God by your side, there is nothing that you can't achieve. Marie is a well-rounded individual who lives with passion, dedication, and grace. Her dream is to ensure prosperity for all.

To connect, email her at HopeTogether@mail.com

Cheryl Polote-Williamson is a global media executive whose purpose is to help people share their stories and attain healing. She is the visionary behind thirteen bestselling books, including *Words from the Spirit for the Spirit*, *Affirmed*, and the Soul Talk series. She holds a bachelor of science in criminal justice and is also a certified life coach and the executive director of the 501(c)(3), Soul Reborn.

Cheryl has amassed numerous accolades such as featured author at the NAACP and Congressional Black Caucus Conference, 2017 winner of the IALA Literary Trailblazer of the Year award, and executive producer of the year for the stage play *Soul Purpose*. In addition, Cheryl's first film production was selected for the Greater Cleveland Urban Film Festival and the BronzeLens Film Festival. Her upcoming projects include *Soulful Prayers, Vol. 2*, and the films *Saving Clarissa* and *Illegal Rose*.

Cheryl resides in Texas with her husband, Russell Williamson Sr. They have three children and two grandchildren.

Learn more at www.cherylpwilliamson.com

BCS Solutions

HOW SECURE IS YOUR CASH FLOW?

www.bcsconsultinggrp.com

Dee Bowden is the founder of BCS Solutions.

BCS Solutions signature process AMENDs your company's collections process, improve your company's revenue so you can focus on the business at hand.

Audit, Meet, Establish, Narrow, Determine (AMEND)

BCS Solutions serves small businesses B2B and B2G by providing a personalized approach to untangle the disconnects in Sales, Contracts, Accounts Payable, and Accounts Receivable which impact the cash flow in your business.

Remember The Sale is Not Complete until the Money is in the Bank and not just on the books!

We Fix Your Financial Disconnects!

instagram.com/bowdendee
facebook.com/dee.bowden.5
linkedin.com/in/dee-bowden-bcssolutions

CREATING DISTINCTIVE BOOKS
WITH INTENTIONAL RESULTS

We're a collaborative group of creative masterminds
with a mission to produce high-quality books to position
you for monumental success in the marketplace.

Our professional team of writers, editors, designers,
and marketing strategists work closely together to ensure
that every detail of your book is a clear representation
of the message in your writing.

Want to know more?
Write to us at info@publishyourgift.com
or call (888) 949-6228

Discover great books, exclusive offers, and more at
www.PublishYourGift.com

Connect with us on social media

@publishyourgift

CPSIA information can be obtained
at www.ICGtesting.com
Printed in the USA
FSHW010056290220
67522FS